STORM PROOF

*100 Days of Triumph
Over Trouble*

STORM PROOF

100 Days of Triumph
Over Trouble

FOREWORD

"I AM the master of the storm. I AM the anchor of your soul. I AM the conqueror of the wind and the waves. I AM the mighty God, the Prince of Peace. And I AM in the boat with you!"

—STORM PROOF: 100 DAYS OF TRIUMPH OVER TROUBLE, DAY 42

Life is amazing. It's a great adventure. It is full of love and blessing and joy. Nevertheless, storms come to everyone. Jesus made that clear in His parable about the two houses, one built on sand and the other built upon a rock-solid foundation.

Laurie and I have certainly faced storms in our lives. And we know there will surely be others in the years to come. The same is true for you and your household. That's why we asked our dear friend Pastor John Hagee, a favorite of our viewers, to create this 100-day devotional to equip us all to navigate the seasons that may lie ahead.

We want you to have that immovable, unshakeable foundation that will ensure your triumph in the coming year. We want to help you experience victory!

With that goal in mind, each day's message will begin with God's Word, revealing the life-changing, storm-stopping promises available for you. You'll learn The Recipe for Peace and how to Face Your Fears, realize that God is Right Where You Are in the midst of the storm, and so much more.

We know storms will come. We also know when the world is crumbling around us, we can count on Him. We can trust Him to teach us what we are to learn in the storm so we are ready for the great blessings He has for us when the storm clears.

—Matt and Laurie Crouch

INTRODUCTION: YOU ARE STORM PROOF

01

"These things I have spoken to you, that in Me you may have peace. In the world you will have tribulation; but be of good cheer, I have overcome the world."

JOHN 16:33

I have spent a lot of time on airplanes in my lifetime. But no matter how many times I fly, I always listen to the flight attendant's instructions. I note where the life vests are, how to fasten my seatbelt and put on my oxygen mask, and most importantly, I look around for the nearest exit. Why do I bother? Because I want to be prepared if trouble comes. When we aren't prepared, we panic. At the slightest turbulence, people will start shouting and giving death-bed confessions. Did you know that panic kills more people in fires than the fire itself? Panic in a crowded room will get people trampled on. Our military and police force are taught not to panic and how to talk people down from panicking, in order to resolve issues peacefully. Panic is a problem of the unprepared.

Jesus wasn't one to mince words. He was very clear in John 16:33: "In this world you will have trouble" (NIV). You will! There is no getting around it. You can't avoid trouble, but you can be prepared for it when it comes. You can be "storm proof." Storm proof doesn't mean you *prevent* storms from happening; it means you triumph over trouble when storms come.

Think about it this way. When you weatherproof your house, you aren't stopping hurricanes, blizzards, and tornadoes from happening. You aren't changing the laws of nature, like Elijah who commanded the rains to fall and then to stop (see 1 Kings 17:1). You aren't going to be looking out your picture window one day and seeing a hailstorm over this neighbor and a flood over that neighbor, all the while you are laying out and getting a suntan. No. You are merely ensuring that your house can stand up to the storms that inevitably come.

The same is true for your life. You can prepare for the turbulence that will inevitably come in your job, your marriage, your relationships, your finances, and your spirit; so when they do come, you don't panic. You won't panic when you fail. You won't panic when you get rejected. You won't give in to fear and anxiety. You won't lose hope if you get sick. You will be prepared! You will be ready to fight back with the tools God has given you because *you are storm proof.*

In the days to come, you will learn how to have peace regardless of your circumstances. You will learn to choose joy when everything is coming against you. You will learn to rejoice in your suffering and find yourself laughing at the devil's schemes. But be prepared! He may try to attack you as you walk through these next 100 days, giving opportunities to put your faith into practice. But each day you will find your faith getting stronger. Because when you fill up on the Word of God, when you spend time in His presence, when you seek His will for your life, when you walk in obedience and love, you are ensuring that your faith can withstand the trials and tribulations of life. Are you ready?

PRAYER

Father, I declare in faith, that with You by my side I can weather any storm. You are my strong tower. You are my protector and defender. You are strength in my weakness. With You in my life, I have nothing to fear because You work all things together for good. In Jesus' name; Amen.

02

"Because he loves me," says the Lord, "I will rescue him; I will protect him, for he acknowledges my name. He will call on me, and I will answer him; I will be with him in trouble, I will deliver him and honor him. With long life I will satisfy him and show him my salvation."

PSALM 91:14–16 NIV

Trouble is the gateway to discovering the power of God, because God Himself cannot deliver the man or the woman who is not in trouble. God cannot show you His power—you will never know God in all His glory—until you get in real trouble.

How can you know God is a healing God without being in a battle with sickness or disease? How can you know God as your provider without having been in need? How can you know that God sticks closer than a brother without having been lonely and rejected, or cast aside by those you love? How can you know that God is a healer of broken hearts unless you have spent the night sobbing in your own personal Gethsemane, when the night seems so long and dark? How can you know God as a deliverer unless you have lived in the chains of captivity?

So, let me ask: Are you in real trouble? If your answer is yes … that's wonderful! It's absolutely thrilling, because you're in the perfect position to discover the God of the Bible— the God who answers prayer, who comforts the brokenhearted, who heals the sick, who restores shattered dreams. You will discover, in the day of trouble, the God who leads you and comforts you. He is the Shepherd through the valley of the shadow of death. He is the God who gives you victory over your enemies.

When you get in trouble, you will discover the God who comes to your rescue. You will discover joy that is unspeakable and full of glory. You will discover the God who gives you hope that is the anchor of your soul, who opens the gates of heaven to the righteous. You will discover Him only when you come into great trouble. And you can rest assured that He will rescue you, because the Bible says that no good thing will He withhold from those who diligently seek Him (see Psalm 84:11). He is greater than the giants you're fighting. He is greater than the mountains you're climbing. He is greater than the burdens you're carrying. "Greater is He who is in you than He who is in the world" (1 John 4:4). Give Him praise!

_____

_____

_____

_____

_____

_____

_____

_____

_____

PRAYER

Father God, I have heard Your Word today. I call upon You in this day of trouble and declare that I will experience the joy of Your victorious deliverance from every storm. I am grateful for the trials I face, as I discover more of who You are— Rescuer, Healer, Deliverer; You are a good, good Father! In Jesus' name; Amen.

IF YOU CALL, HE WILL ANSWER

03

"Call upon Me in the day of trouble; I will deliver you, and you shall glorify Me."

PSALM 50:15

In today's scripture verse, David reminds us to call upon God in times of trouble. As powerful as God is, God cannot answer your prayers until you pray them.

Throughout my entire life as a pastor, I have had people come into my office to tell me their problems. My first response is always, "Have you prayed about it?" And so often they say, "No." They were waiting for me to do something about it for them!

Hear this: prayer *is* doing something about it. You involve God when you pray about it. When you pray about it, Jesus Christ, who is your intermediary, makes sure that your prayer is recorded in the chronicles of heaven.

Matthew 18:18 says, "Assuredly, I say to you, whatever you bind on earth will be bound in heaven, and whatever you loose on earth will be loosed in heaven." Supernatural powers come into play when you pray. God begins to answer what you think can't be answered. He starts to control what you think is out of control. He does the impossible in your life, and suddenly the storm clouds are gone because we serve a prayer-answering God!

When the three Hebrew boys were in the fiery furnace, they called upon the Lord and the fourth man appeared in the flames. When you get in trouble, God does not send someone to help you, He shows up!

Imagine that you are a king or queen of unlimited wealth and you see a ragged, hungry, starving child begging in the streets. You say to that child: "Call on me tomorrow at the palace and I will give you every desire of your heart; this is my royal decree." The next day, the child comes to the palace and presents the royal decree to you with a face full of hope and expectation. Wouldn't you help that child? Of course you would! Jesus Christ, the King of Glory, the King of unlimited wealth and power, the Creator of heaven and earth, has written a royal decree to His children called the Word of God, and in it He says: "Call upon me in the day of trouble; I will deliver you."

God's proposition is simple: if you call, He will answer. It really is that easy!

PRAYER

Heavenly Father, in the name of the Lord Jesus Christ, I call upon You, the God of Abraham, Isaac, and Jacob, to deliver me in the day of trouble. I know that You are the Almighty God. I know that You hear me, and that You will answer. And so today, in faith, I receive Your answer for my trouble. Even though I may not see it with my natural eyes, with wings of faith, my answer is coming. You are my Deliverer! In Jesus' name; Amen.

04

And He said to me, "My grace is sufficient for you, for My strength is made perfect in weakness." Therefore most gladly I will rather boast in my infirmities, that the power of Christ may rest upon me.

2 CORINTHIANS 12:9

Any time a storm arises, our first instinct is to ask God to take it away. Take away the hurt. Take away the betrayal. Take away the cancer. Take away the infidelity. Take away the gossip. Take away the unkind words. Take away the mistake that caused this storm in the first place.

Jesus asked the same thing of God the night before He was crucified: "... please take this cup of suffering away from me" (Luke 22:42 NLT). Please, God, take it away! But Jesus' prayer didn't end there, and neither should ours. Jesus continued: "... Yet I want your will to be done, not mine." God had a plan for the storm that Jesus found Himself in. God can use our storms too.

The Apostle Paul wrote that he asked God THREE TIMES to take away the "thorn in the flesh" that was causing him so much suffering. But there was so much of God's power flowing through Paul that God refused to remove his weakness. God was essentially saying to him, "If I remove that weakness, people will begin to think of you as God, and you might get to the place where you believe it yourself."

> *And lest I should be exalted above measure by the abundance of the revelations, a thorn in the flesh was given to me, a messenger of Satan to buffet me, lest I be exalted above measure. Concerning this thing I pleaded with the Lord three times that it might depart from me. And He said to me, "My grace is sufficient for you, for*

My strength is made perfect in weakness." Therefore most gladly I will rather boast in my infirmities, that the power of Christ may rest upon me. Therefore I take pleasure in infirmities, in reproaches, in needs, in persecutions, in distresses, for Christ's sake. For when I am weak, then I am strong (2 Corinthians 12:7–10).

Any time we think we are strong enough, smart enough, wealthy enough, connected enough—any time we think we are "enough" without God—we are saying that we don't need Him in our lives. Yet, He uses our weaknesses, our failures, our faults, our storms to show Himself strong. Just look at the lives of some of the greatest preachers in history. George Whitfield, whose ministry led to the development of the Methodist Church, preached with asthma. Smith Wigglesworth, a great healing evangelist, suffered from kidney stones. Charles Spurgeon, prince of all preachers, died with gout before he turned sixty. Jonathan Edwards was so near-sighted that when he read his great sermon, "Sinners in the Hands of an Angry God," ink from the page rubbed off on his face and turned his nose black. None of these ministers of the Gospel had their thorns removed, but they didn't let that stop them. They trusted God to be the strength in their weakness, grace where they needed it most, the rose among thorns.

PRAYER

God, You are the strength in my weakness. Your grace is sufficient for all my needs. Show me, Lord, what You want to teach me in this storm. Not my will, but Yours be done. In Jesus' name; Amen.

STICKS AND STONES

05

Do not let any unwholesome talk come out of your mouths, but only what is helpful for building others up according to their needs, that it may benefit those who listen.

EPHESIANS 4:29 NIV

Going out to meet trouble is life's shortest walk. If you're not in trouble today, you're headed for trouble. That's not being negative; that is being realistic. There are all kinds of ways we get ourselves into trouble. One key way we get into trouble is by what we say.

The story is told of a man who went to his company business party. Being naïve, he drank too much of the spiked punch. He went home very drunk and woke up the next morning with a splitting headache. When he managed to open his eyes, he saw two aspirin sitting on his bedside table. He took them to the bathroom to get a drink of water and saw in the mirror that he had a black eye. He found a note from his wife that read, "Sweetheart, your breakfast is on the kitchen table: bacon, eggs, toast, jelly, coffee, everything you like. I've gone shopping for your favorite foods for supper. Be back soon, your loving wife." The man found his son and asked, "What happened last night?" The son said, "Dad, you came home at three o'clock this morning, falling down drunk. You fell onto the coffee table and walked right into a door, which probably explains that black eye. Mom tried to help you get undressed to go to bed when you started screaming, "Leave me alone! I'm a married man!" Ha! Give the Lord a shout! Saying the right thing at the right time will get you out of trouble every time. Can I get an "Amen!"

King Solomon, the wisest man who ever lived, wrote Proverbs, an entire book devoted to this idea.

A soft answer turns away wrath, but a harsh word stirs up anger. The tongue of the wise uses knowledge rightly, but the mouth of fools pours forth foolishness. The eyes of the LORD are in every place, keeping watch on the evil and the good. A wholesome tongue is a tree of life, but perverseness in it breaks the spirit (Proverbs 15:1–4).

The heart of the wise teaches his mouth, and adds learning to his lips. Pleasant words are like a honeycomb, sweetness to the soul and health to the bones (Proverbs 16:23–24).

A word fitly spoken is like apples of gold in settings of silver (Proverbs 25:11).

Telling lies about others is as harmful as hitting them with an ax, wounding them with a sword, or shooting them with a sharp arrow (Proverbs 25:18 NLT).

The wisest man in all the world knew how important the words are that we speak. Sticks and stones may not break your bones, but words can hurt. So, work hard to say the right thing at the right time. Be honest with your speech. Be quick to forgive and to ask for forgiveness. Do not lie or let any unwholesome talk come from your mouth. Pray for a wise tongue and it will keep you out of trouble!

PRAYER

Lord, I declare that I will use my words wisely, to build others up, to forgive, to speak truth and honesty. If I am about to say something I shouldn't, I ask You to muzzle me in the name of the Lord! Amen.

HOW TO TRIUMPH
IN THE DAY OF TROUBLE

06

*In all your ways
acknowledge
Him, and He
shall direct your
paths.*

PROVERBS 3:6

In John 10, Jesus speaks about being the Shepherd of the sheep. He says: "I am the good shepherd. The good shepherd gives His life for the sheep" (v. 11). Later in the chapter, He speaks directly of the sheep: "My sheep hear My voice, and I know them, and they follow Me" (v. 27). Jesus is the Good Shepherd; we are the sheep. As His flock, we can hear His voice. We can discern His voice from all others: "... the sheep follow him, for they know his voice. Yet they will by no means follow a stranger, but will flee from him, for they do not know the voice of strangers" (vv. 4–5). How do we know His voice? By spending time with Him. By reading His Word. In prayer.

Prayer is a two-way street. It is taking your concerns to God, and it is listening for His voice. The more you exercise your prayer life, the more able you are to discern His voice from the wolves. How many times have you heard someone say, "I've tried everything else; I've got nothing left to do but pray"? How many times have you said it yourself? My friend, prayer should be your first choice, not your last chance. In John 14:13, Jesus said, "Whatever you ask in My name, that I will do, that the Father may be glorified in the Son." Whatever you ask in Jesus' name, He will do it. You just have to ask!

Let me tell you something: when you really start to do something that counts for God, the devil will line up his troops to knock you off track. And on the other side of the line of scrimmage, swiftly will come the Lord of hosts with all His delegated force, and He will scatter your enemies like the straw of the summer threshing floor—*if you ask Him to.* Let me tell you, I know that to be true!

Notice that John 10:27 says the sheep hear the shepherd's voice "and they follow Me." Walking in obedience is not just being able to recognize God's voice, it is recognizing His voice AND following Him. If you are in a day of trouble, you can triumph by heeding the voice of God. If you don't immediately hear Him, do the last thing He told you to do and keep doing that until you hear a new word. Seek wise counsel; spend time in the Scriptures; spend time in prayer; and He will redirect you until you are back on track. Proverbs 3:6 (NLT) says, "Seek his will in all you do, and he will show you which path to take." Trust Him; He will show you which path to take. That's how you triumph in the day of trouble!

PRAYER

Heavenly Father, I expect that when I ask, You will send. I expect that my advocate in heaven, Jesus Christ, will present my petition to You and You will dispatch Your angels to this earth to carry out that assignment. Thank you for making my paths straight and leading me to triumph in my day of trouble! In Jesus' name; Amen.

GOD IS RIGHT WHERE YOU ARE

07

*And it shall
come to pass
that whoever
calls on the
name of the
LORD shall be
saved. For in
Mount Zion and
in Jerusalem
there shall be
deliverance, as
the LORD has
said, among the
remnant whom
the LORD calls.*

JOEL 2:32

The Bible says that "... 'Everyone who calls on the name of the LORD will be saved'" (Romans 10:13 NLT). It doesn't say everyone who calls from a stained-glass cathedral will be saved, or everyone who calls from their great-granddaddy's church, or everyone who wears their Sunday best, or everyone who calls from the confession box, or everyone who calls on their knees, or everyone worthy of calling upon Him will be saved. It simply says *everyone*—no matter who you are, where you are, or what you've done—you can call on Him and be saved. No matter who you are, what you've done, God is right where you are!

Jonah called from the belly of a whale, and God showed up. God heard his prayer, even through all that blubber.

Elijah called while in a deep depression from the brook called Cherith, hiding from Jezebel because she was killing men of God. Elijah called, and God showed up. God showed up in the form of angels sent to feed Elijah some homemade angel food cake. That cake was all the nourishment he needed. Elijah got up and ran 40 miles, racing past the king's chariot, because he was energized by the power and presence of God. Think about that. The king's horses were the fastest, best fed horses in the country and Elijah ran 40 miles in front of them. That's Holy Spirit power!

Paul and Silas called from a Roman prison. The angels shook that jail off its foundation. "Jailhouse Rock" did not start with Elvis Presley;

it started with Paul and Silas. They walked out of that jail with the jailhouse keys in one hand and a convert in the other, because God heard them behind the walls of a prison. You may be reading this from the penitentiary right now. If you are, I want you to know: God has not given up on you. Don't you give up on God! He hears you!

Jew, Gentile, slave, free, male, female, child, elderly, no matter your race, education level, or political affiliation, God saves *everyone* who calls on Him. "For God so loved the world that He gave His only begotten Son, that **whoever** believes in Him should not perish but have everlasting life" (John 3:16, emphasis added).

PRAYER

God, I believe that everyone who calls on You will be saved from the power of sin and darkness. Your power is mighty to bring down strongholds. Your power breaks the chains of misery and the havoc that enslaves us. You heal sick bodies, minds, and souls, because You are the Great Physician, the Balm of Gilead. You restore marriages and return prodigals to their parents. You are the Prince of Peace, the Everlasting Father, our Mighty Counselor. You are from everlasting to everlasting; there is none like You in all the earth. Through Your sacrifice I know that whoever believes in You will not perish but have everlasting life. In Jesus' name; Amen.

WHO IS THIS GOD?

08

The Mighty One, God the LORD, has spoken and called the earth from the rising of the sun to its going down.

Who is this God who says, "Call upon Me"? He is *Elohim*, the Mighty One, the Mighty God of Israel. When you address the Mighty God of Israel, God extends His ear suddenly. There is power in His name: "From the rising of the sun to its going down the LORD'S name is to be praised" (Psalm 113:3). The name "Rockefeller" will open the doors of finance all over the world. The name "Einstein" will open the doors of science. The name "Beethoven" will open the doors of music halls. And the name "Jesus" will open the doors of heaven and close the gates of hell. His name is above every name. His name!

Isaiah called Him, "Wonderful, Counselor, Mighty God, Everlasting Father, Prince of Peace" (Isaiah 9:6). Mary called Him "Jesus, for He will save His people from their sins" (Matthew 1:21). I call Him Lord and Savior, Friend, Deliverer, Counselor, and my comforter. In the day of battle, He is my shield and buckler. He is my fortress and my high tower. He is the Rock in the weary land from which the waters flow that refresh and restore. He is the Great I AM. He is the Great Physician who heals. He is the Great Shepherd who guides and provides.

Who is this God? He is the Alpha and the Omega, the beginning and the end, the first and the last. He is the Bread of Life. He is honey in the rock. He is meat for men. He is milk for children. He is the Cornerstone, precious and elect in Zion. He is *Emmanuel*, "God With Us," the hope of glory. He is the fountain filled with blood drawn from *Emmanuel's* vein. He is the immortal, invisible God. He is the Lion of the

15 | JOHN HAGEE

tribe of Judah. He is the Lord of glory and the Light of the world. He is the Lamb of God!

> And it happened, as He was alone praying, that His disciples joined Him, and He asked them, saying, "Who do the crowds say that I am?" So they answered and said, "John the Baptist, but some say Elijah; and others say that one of the old prophets has risen again." He said to them, "But who do you say that I am?" Peter answered and said, "The Christ of God" (Luke 9:18–20).

PRAYER

Mighty God of Israel, Your name is above all names. There is power in Your name and that name is to be praised. In the storms of life, I know that I can call upon Your name, Jehovah Jireh, and You will see me and meet my every need. I come to You in the power of Jesus' name; Amen!

09

In the beginning God created the heavens and the earth. The earth was without form, and void; and darkness was on the face of the deep. And the Spirit of God was hovering over the face of the waters.

GENESIS 1:1–2

Creation was God's power on parade. The earth did not evolve; it was created by the spoken word of God. He gathered a lump of dirt and breathed into it, and man became a living soul. He didn't rearrange what was already here. He created something—all things—out of nothing. Joyce Kilmer was a great poet. In her poem titled *Trees*, she wrote, "Poems are made by fools like me, but only God can make a tree." I sometimes think God needs a public relations firm to go around hanging signs on trees that say, "This tree has been placed here by the courtesy of the Almighty."

Atheists and agnostics, pseudo-intellectuals, progressives, all believe that billions of years ago the sun shone on a pool of stagnant water and a tadpole started to wiggle. After millions of years, it crawled out on land and developed a tail. Then, it learned how to walk. After a few more million years, it climbed a tree and hung by its tail. And, that is your great-great-granddaddy.

I don't believe that. I don't believe that you believe that. I believe God scooped up a handful of dirt, breathed into it, and man became a living soul. "And the LORD God formed man of the dust of the ground, and breathed into his nostrils the breath of life; and man became a living being" (Genesis 2:7). The Word is the *ruach* of God, which in Hebrew means "breath, wind, spirit." The Spirit of God lives in you! He gave you your first breath.

In the Genesis of time, God breathed into a handful of dirt, and Adam became a living soul.

God separated the day from the night. He flung the glittering stars against the velvety night sky to glisten like diamonds as an eternal reminder to mankind that He is the infinite Creator. He set the sun ablaze and placed it in the heavens as His version of the eternal flame. He holds the seven seas in the palm of His hand. He is the Shepherd who calls the stars—over fifty million galaxies worth—by name. The infinite power of God to create is far beyond what we can grasp or understand. The God of the Bible is a God of might and miracles. He's a God of grace and glory. The God we serve is the God of power, more power than the world can possibly imagine.

> The earth is the LORD'S, and all its fullness, the world and those who dwell therein. For He has founded it upon the seas, and established it upon the waters (Psalm 24:1–2).

PRAYER

Lord, no weapon against me can prosper because I have You—the Creator of the universe and everything in it—on my side. The Spirit of God lives within me by Your very breath. Everywhere I look I see Your power on parade. I praise Your holy name! In Jesus' name I pray; Amen.

LET TROUBLE BRING OUT
THE BEST IN YOU

10

*It is good for me
that I have been
afflicted, that I
may learn Your
statutes.*

PSALM 119:71

God can turn affliction into a means to success. Consider Helen Keller: she graduated from college with honors, even though she was blind and deaf. Or Glenn Cunningham, who had over ninety-percent of his body burned in a schoolhouse fire when he was a child. Doctors said he would never walk again. Yet, he not only learned to walk again, but he began to run. He discovered that because the nerves in his legs had been damaged, they didn't hurt when he pushed himself to the limit. He didn't stop pushing himself until he'd broken the world record for the fastest mile. He took his troubles and became a world champion because of it.

And what about Jesus Christ of Nazareth? He was a minority. Some called him "illegitimate." He was called a heretic by the Church, a traitor by the State. He was called a drunkard, and a demonized teacher. (Not exactly great credentials for a minister.) Yet, He took all those troubles and turned them into triumphs when He took all our sins to the Cross.

Trouble is an asset. We hate trouble. We run from it. We complain about trouble. But the truth is, trouble has made you who you are. Dr. D.K. Olukoya said, "What a man needs to get ahead in life is a powerful enemy." When Jesus talks about loving our enemies in Matthew 5, Eugene Peterson's translation says, "Let them bring out the best in you, not the worst" (Matthew 5:44 MSG). Our antagonist is our helper; it strengthens our muscles and sharpens our wit. Our antagonist develops our skill. It transforms your spaghetti spine into steel.

What does that? T-R-O-U-B-L-E. Trouble!
James wrote,

> My brethren, count it all joy when you fall into various trials, knowing that the testing of your faith produces patience. But let patience have its perfect work, that you may be perfect and complete, lacking nothing (James 1:2–4).

Count it all joy! How? Why? Because trouble has the potential to bring out the best in you—it produces patience and perfection so that you lack nothing. So have a joy explosion and watch the darkest hour of your life dissipate into a radiant dawn!

PRAYER

God, You have given us the license to be a joyous, happy, victorious, prosperous people, even in the midst of our storms. I am determined to take advantage of who You say I am in the body of Christ—patient under fire, learning through my trials, allowing my adversaries to bring out the best in me. I am who You say I am! In Jesus' name; Amen.

TROUBLE UNDER PRESSURE

11

We are hard-pressed on every side, yet not crushed; we are perplexed, but not in despair; persecuted, but not forsaken; struck down, but not destroyed.

2 CORINTHIANS 4:8–9

Do you know the difference between a priceless diamond and a lump of coal? A diamond is a lump of coal that was made good under pressure. The trouble it endured made its value seen. God likewise permits trouble to develop you.

Saint Paul wrote in 2 Corinthians 4:8, "We are troubled on every side ..." (KJV). Trouble is coming from the north, south, east, and west, from Christians and non-Christians alike. We've got big trouble, Paul says, but we won't let that stop us! "... we are perplexed, but not in despair; persecuted, but not forsaken; struck down, but not destroyed" (v. 9), because we serve a God who is bigger than all the trouble of the world; and we are victorious in the name that is above every name!

In John 14:27, Jesus said: "Peace I leave with you, My peace I give to you; not as the world gives do I give to you. Let not your heart be troubled, neither let it be afraid." You can have "the peace of God, which surpasses all understanding" (Philippians 4:7) even in the midst of your troubles, knowing that "I [you] can do all things through Christ who strengthens me [you]" (v. 13).

It helps me to think of trouble as simply "resistance." Without the resistance of wind, a bird cannot fly. Without the resistance of water, a massive ship cannot float. Without the resistance of gravity, you could not walk. The petals of a flower do not yield their perfume until they've been crushed. An olive will not yield its oil until it is pulverized. Trouble is the womb where greatness is birthed. It is resistance, pressure, and trouble that allows us to become more like Christ.

Eugene Peterson's translation of the Bible, *The Message*, says this: "God brings the best out of you, develops well-formed maturity in you" (Romans 12:2 MSG). People who follow the world's ways want an easy life, free from trouble, but that is not how maturity is developed. Maturity is developed in God's university of adversity. He strengthens us in our troubles to make us more valuable to the Kingdom of God. Jesus proved His Sonship by being strong, patient, compassionate, forgiving, loving, and perfect through ever trial and persecution He faced. When we can face life's greatest challenges with the mindset that "all things work together for good to those who love God, to those who are the called according to His purpose" (Romans 8:28), we become more like Jesus.

Are you in trouble? God is shaping you to reach your destiny!

PRAYER

Father God, I believe that You are with me in times of trouble, transforming my life's difficulties into priceless diamonds. You are going to deliver me in the day of trouble, and from that trouble birth Your destiny in my life. I am not afraid. I am not dismayed. God of heaven, You are with me. In Jesus' name; Amen.

THE SPIRITUAL HARD OF HEARING

12

And after the earthquake a fire; but the LORD was not in the fire: and after the fire a still small voice.

1 KINGS 19:12 KJV

There was a woman who went to her pastor and said, "Pastor, my husband has a problem. He never hears a thing I say." The pastor said, "That's not a problem; that's a spiritual gift!"

Some of us in the church have that problem. We tune God out until He has to turn it up. Face it, we humans are spiritually hard of hearing, so sometimes God has to turn it up until we take notice! One way that God turns it up in the Bible is through earthquakes. There was an earthquake on Resurrection morning that opened the grave—not to let Jesus out, but to let us in to see He had risen, and was going to the right hand of the Father:

> *And behold, there was a great earthquake; for an angel of the Lord descended from heaven, and came and rolled back the stone from the door, and sat on it. His countenance was like lightning, and his clothing as white as snow. And the guards shook for fear of him, and became like dead men* (Matthew 28:2–4).

There was an earthquake that set Paul and Silas free from the Philippian jail:

> *But at midnight Paul and Silas were praying and singing hymns to God, and the prisoners were listening to them. Suddenly there was a great earthquake, so that the foundations of the prison were shaken; and immediately all the doors were opened and everyone's chains were loosed* (Acts 16:25–26).

The Book of Revelation is full of earthquakes,

as God announces the tribulation:

I looked when He opened the sixth seal, and behold, there was a great earthquake; and the sun became black as sackcloth of hair, and the moon became like blood. And the stars of heaven fell to the earth, as a fig tree drops its late figs when it is shaken by a mighty wind. Then the sky receded as a scroll when it is rolled up, and every mountain and island was moved out of its place. And the kings of the earth, the great men, the rich men, the commanders, the mighty men, every slave and every free man, hid themselves in the caves and in the rocks of the mountains, and said to the mountains and rocks, "Fall on us and hide us from the face of Him who sits on the throne and from the wrath of the Lamb! For the great day of His wrath has come, and who is able to stand?" (Revelation 6:12–17).

Hear me: God is in charge. He is not a doting imbecile sitting benignly in the heavens, out of touch and out of control. He is not wringing His hands over the acts of the ungodly. The Bible says, "He who sits in the heavens shall laugh" (Psalm 2:4). God is giving a harsh laugh. He's not concerned about armies, atomic power, riches or wealth. He can snatch it away quicker than dust can hit the ground. He is not threatened by the rich and the powerful. For every knee is going to bow and every tongue is going to confess that Jesus Christ is Lord to the glory of God the Father.

PRAYER

Heavenly Father, I tune my ears to You. Speak to me! Whether You speak through the roar of an earthquake or a still small voice, I will listen. In Jesus' name; Amen.

IRRITATE THE DEVIL

13

Blessed are you when they revile and persecute you, and say all kinds of evil against you falsely for My sake. Rejoice and be exceedingly glad, for great is your reward in heaven, for so they persecuted the prophets who were before you.

MATTHEW 5:11–12

There is nothing that irritates the devil more than when we laugh at his tactics. In Matthew 5, during His Sermon on the Mount, Jesus told the people to be prepared, because as followers of The Way, others would attempt to discredit Jesus by discrediting them.

Others will lie to you and about you. They will spread rumors and "say all kinds of evil against you falsely." They will put you down. They will insult you, mock you, mistreat you, and persecute you.

And how are we to respond when that happens? Jesus said we should "rejoice and be exceedingly glad." Ha! Take that devil! *Oh, hallelujah; they are talking about me again! They've told another big lie about me again! Yahoo! Putting me down? That must mean God is doing something big in my life that is making the devil mad!* Don't let steam come out of your ears. Get happy that you're doing something that irritates the devil enough for him to make one of his little disciples start running their mouth about you. When the devil comes at you, you can ask him: *Is that all you've got? Well, I can one-up you every day of the week; because I've got Jesus and, together, we are rejoicing in heaven every time you attack! Ha!*

Society needs to take a page from Jesus' book. People are so easily offended these days. But James said, "You must understand this, my beloved: let everyone be quick to listen, slow to speak, slow to anger" (James 1:19, NRSV). Slow to respond; friends, s-l-o-w to anger. And

Solomon, in all his wisdom, wrote: "He who is slow to anger is better than the mighty, and he who rules his spirit than he who takes a city" (Proverbs 16:32). Don't let the devil provoke you. Provoke him by keeping your peace rather than losing your lid, and you will always come out on top!

In Matthew 25:21, Jesus said: "... Enter into the joy of your lord." You enter into the joy of the Lord when you exercise your faith. You move toward joy when you practice keeping your peace. You enter into joy when you respond to the devil's schemes with Jesus' foolproof remedy: "Rejoice, and be exceedingly glad: for great is your reward in heaven ..." (KJV). Yes, and amen!

PRAYER

When others mistreat me, I will remember that they are not my enemy, Satan is! And in Your strength, I can rejoice and be glad, because You have overcome the devil and all his tactics. No weapon formed against me shall prosper. No insults, no rumors, no lies stand a chance against the joy of the Lord. Hallelujah! In Jesus' name; Amen.

JOY IN THE DAY OF TROUBLE

14

The blessing of the LORD makes one rich, and He adds no sorrow with it.

PROVERBS 10:22

Christianity was born in the spirit of joy. If we lose our joy, we've lost our Christian credentials. The church of Jesus Christ must rediscover its joy. Our marriages, our homes, our workplaces, our devotional times must be refreshed by a joy explosion.

Can we have joy in the day of trouble? According to the Word of God, yes. Jesus Christ, just hours before He was plunged into the sea of suffering at the Cross of Calvary, where His body was going to be ripped apart by the Roman government, looked at His disciples and said: "These things I have spoken to you, that My joy may remain in you, and that your joy may be full" (John 15:11). One of Jesus' final messages before His death was about the fullness of joy!

When David danced before the Lord in a joyful celebration for what God had done in bringing the Ark of the Covenant back to Israel, his wife looked down on him from a second story window and mocked him. God cursed David's wife on the spot and made her barren for the rest of her life. Barrenness was the most severe curse in the Old Testament. Our churches are barren because we have rejected the joy of the Lord that "maketh rich and addeth no sorrow" (KJV). America is sick and tired of what I call "sourpuss Christianity." If you're walking around looking like a bulldog baptized in lemon juice, you're not deep, you're not super spiritual, you simply don't even know God. You need to get saved.

Saint Paul nailed it when he said, "Rejoice in the Lord always: and again I say, Rejoice" (Philippians 4:4). We have every reason to be fixed with a joy that is unshakeable. Many of you need to experience an old-fashioned, spirit-filled joy explosion so unspeakable and full of glory where you can shout for joy and know that God is with you regardless of your circumstances. Paul didn't say "rejoice when everything is going your way" or "rejoice when your trouble is over." No, he said, "Rejoice in the Lord always: and again I say, Rejoice." He knew he had to repeat himself for you to get it. Rejoice! Rejoice, in God your Savior!

How many of you are in a time of trouble, and you want to move toward the joy of the Lord that "maketh rich and addeth no sorrow?" I don't care what your trouble is, you can have joy in the midst of it because God says you can.

PRAYER

Lord Jesus Christ, I declare a joy explosion over my life. You have promised me joy all the days of my life; You "maketh rich and addeth no sorrow." Today, I surrender all my hurts and hang-ups and negative emotions to You and replace them with rejoicing. Today, I declare joy even in my day of trouble. In Jesus' name; Amen and Amen.

THREE CHEERS FROM JESUS

15

But immediately Jesus spoke to them, saying, "Be of good cheer! It is I; do not be afraid."

MATTHEW 14:27

Hip, hip, hooray! Jesus gives us three cheers to encourage us to triumph in our day of trouble.

In John 15, Jesus begins a long discussion with His disciples about what lies ahead. He told them that the world is going to hate them just like the world hates Him. And that they will be persecuted just like the world persecutes Him (see John 15:18–25). Not much of a pep talk! But He continues in the next chapter, telling them that He is saying all these things to encourage them, so that when trouble comes they won't give up or stumble, but they will remember what Jesus said and know that He is the Son of the Living God and that they had been with Him. He tells them He is going away, but the Holy Spirit will come to comfort them. He knows that they don't yet fully understand and will see this as sad news, so He says: "These things I have spoken to you, that in Me you may have peace. In the world you will have tribulation; but be of good cheer, I have overcome the world" (John 16:33). "Be of good cheer, I have overcome the world." Hip, hip, hooray! That's the first "good cheer" in our times of trouble!

Our second and third "good cheer" from Jesus shows up in the Gospel of Matthew. Jesus had been going from village to village, healing people. His reputation preceded Him. One day, a group of believers in His own town carried a man to Jesus to be healed of paralysis (see Matthew 9:1):

Then behold, they brought to Him a paralytic lying on a bed. When Jesus saw their faith, He said to the paralytic, "Son, be of good cheer; your sins are forgiven you" (Matthew 9:2).

"... be of good cheer; thy sins be forgiven thee" (KJV). This healing is of importance because it took place in Jesus' own town, where believers were few and far between:

> *... But Jesus said to them, "A prophet is not without honor except in his own country and in his own house." Now He did not do many mighty works there because of their unbelief* (Matthew 13:57–58).

Jesus was moved by the unexpected faith of His neighbors and did something shocking: He didn't immediately heal the man of his paralysis. First, Jesus forgave the man of his sin, *then* told him to get up and walk. Good cheer!

The third "good cheer" from Jesus comes to the disciples as Jesus is walking on water toward their boat at night. They are afraid, thinking He must be a ghost: "But immediately Jesus spoke to them, saying, 'Be of good cheer! It is I; do not be afraid'" (Matthew 14:27).

Be of good cheer. Fear not; it is Jesus. Do not be afraid of the world, the flesh, or the devil. Be of good cheer; He has overcome the world. Be of good cheer; He has forgiven thee. Be of good cheer!

PRAYER

Hip, hip, hooray! Three good cheers from Jesus! Jesus, You have overcome the world and all its tribulations. You took my sins to the Cross and left them there. With You in my corner, I never have to be afraid again. I can even walk on water with You as my Guide! Good cheer! In Jesus' name; Amen.

LOOK BEYOND YOUR CIRCUMSTANCES

16

*This is the day
the LORD has
made; we will
rejoice and be
glad in it.*

PSALM 118:24

Imagine the scene: shepherds, minding their own business, watching their flocks by night, when out of nowhere an angel blazes his way into their pasture.

> *Now there were in the same country shepherds living out in the fields, keeping watch over their flock by night. And behold, an angel of the Lord stood before them, and the glory of the Lord shone around them, and they were greatly afraid. Then the angel said to them, "Do not be afraid, for behold, I bring you good tidings of great joy which will be to all people. For there is born to you this day in the city of David a Savior, who is Christ the Lord. And this will be the sign to you: You will find a Babe wrapped in swaddling cloths, lying in a manger"* (Luke 2:8–12).

Across town, some wise guys from the east had come to Jerusalem, believing that if they followed the star it would point them to the Christ Child: "When they saw the star, they rejoiced with exceedingly great joy" (Matthew 2:10).

Both shepherds and magi experienced this good news, this great joy, and yet the circumstances that surrounded them were not joyful. They lived under the iron fist of the Roman Empire. It was a day of trouble for all the Jews. Romans had crucified 2000 men in one day just to prove their strength as a terrorist state. But when the shepherds heard the word from heavenly angels concerning the birth of Christ, and the wise men saw the star in the sky, they looked beyond their circumstances and were overcome with exceedingly great joy.

I want you to look beyond your trouble, because God is on the throne. God knows who you are. He knows where you are. I want you to look beyond your sickness, because the Healer walks among you. He even makes house calls if you'll call on Him! I want you to look beyond your tears. I want you to look beyond your broken heart, into the darkest night of your life, and know that joy cometh in the morning: "For His anger is but for a moment, His favor is for life; weeping may endure for a night, but joy comes in the morning" (Psalm 30:5). I want you to look beyond the rejection and the bitterness of your past and dare to experience joy.

Quit thinking about every unhappy thing that has happened to you over the last 40 years. Everyone has a sob song that people are tired of listening to! Get over yourself. Inform yourself of this fact: God loves you and everything is going to be all right.

PRAYER

God, today I'm walking away from bitter memories, from resentment, from the hatred of the past to the beautiful things You have for me this day and for the rest of my life. I choose to look beyond my circumstances and declare exceedingly great joy—super joy—in my life! I know that everything is going to be all right. In Jesus' name; Amen.

HE STILL MOVES MOUNTAINS

17

Now to Him who is able to keep you from stumbling, and to present you faultless before the presence of His glory with exceeding joy, to God our Savior, who alone is wise, be glory and majesty, dominion and power, both now and forever. Amen.

JUDE 1:24–25

Where do people get the idea that God no longer performs miracles? That He was strong, performed miracles, and was the all-powerful Creator of the universe for a small period of history? That is not biblical! The Bible says that "Jesus Christ is the same yesterday, today, and forever" (Hebrews 13:8).It says that His glory and majesty and dominion and power are both now AND forever (see Jude 1:25). He still moves mountains and He will move them for you. In fact, He moves them *through* you!

Jesus said,

> *"... nothing will be impossible for you"* (Matthew 17:20).

> *"... He who is in you is greater than he that is in the world"* (1 John 4:4).

> *"Ask, and it will be given to you; seek, and you will find; knock, and the door will be opened to you"* (Matthew 7:7).

> *"Most assuredly, I say to you, he who believes in Me, the works that I do he will do also; and greater works than these he will do, because I go to My Father. And whatever you ask in My name, that I will do, that the Father may be glorified in the Son. If you ask anything in My name, I will do it"* (John 14:12–14).

You can walk into the holy of holies and be in the presence of the living God, the Creator who spoke the stars into existence, who flung the sun and the moon into its place, who scooped up a handful of dirt and breathed into it and man became a living soul. God is the One who has bid you to call upon Him so He can demonstrate His power to you. He can make a way when other people can't. He can move mountains of impossibility. He can divide the waters of the Red Sea and the Jordan River. He can walk through the flames of the fiery furnace with the three Hebrews (Shadrach, Meshach, and Abednego), and He can walk through any fire that you're facing. He closed the mouths of lions for Daniel, and He can do it for you. He can anoint your head with oil. Your cup will run over with an abundance that you can't handle. In your darkest night, when your heart is broken, when you've lost the love of your life, when you've tried and failed, when all hope seems lost, in a daring act of faith, practice the secret of Christian joy: Rejoice in the Lord always. Count it all joy. Have joy in all circumstances. Joy to the Lord! Joy, joy, joy!

PRAYER

Jesus, I believe that You still move mountains and that You will move this mountain for me. You are opening doors, dividing seas, conquering enemies, and I am going to be victorious! Everything is going to be all right. Hallelujah to the Lamb of God! In Jesus' name; Amen.

HAPPINESS AND JOY

18

For David says concerning Him: "I foresaw the LORD always before my face, for He is at my right hand, that I may not be shaken. Therefore my heart rejoiced, and my tongue was glad; moreover my flesh also will rest in hope. For You will not leave my soul in Hades, nor will You allow Your Holy One to see corruption. You have made known to me the ways of life; You will make me full of joy in Your presence."

ACTS 2:25–28

Very few people know the difference between joy and happiness. Most people use the phrase, "I just want to be happy." And they pursue it with drugs, alcohol, sexual fantasies, or exotic trips. And when they get to Shangri-La, they unpack their bags and look in the mirror and discover that the source of all their trouble is looking right back at them. Suddenly their happiness dissipates. It's gone.

The word *happiness* comes from the Scandinavian word *hap* from which we get *happenstance*, meaning "being controlled by circumstance or what happens to you." You're happy because the sun is shining. You're happy because someone complimented you. You're happy because you lost five pounds. You're happy because you don't have to work today, or Valentine's Day is coming, or it's your birthday. You are controlled by what happens to you. Your happiness depends on what happens.

But joy, God's joy, is there no matter what happens. That's the difference. That's the secret to true, Christian joy. It is not based on circumstances, but in believing God is who He says He is and that He will do what He says He will do.

Look at David, a young shepherd boy who was invited to the palace to play soothing music for King Saul. King Saul was plagued by a spirit of distress that tormented him and the only thing that could calm him down was David's harp playing. However, as David grew in prominence, slaying Goliath and tens of thousands of others, Saul's jealousy got the best of him. While David was playing his harp one afternoon, King Saul threw a javelin at David and tried to kill him; but David just kept playing. Most musicians would have run away; but the circumstances didn't matter to David, because his joy in the Lord kept the music coming.

Your circumstances today may not be happy, but God's joy will keep the music coming. Rejoice in the Lord always. Rejoice in the good times. Rejoice in the bad times. Rejoice when you're on the mountaintop. Rejoice when you're walking through the valley of the shadow of death. "Rejoice in the Lord always. Again I will say, rejoice!" (Philippians 4:4).

PRAYER

Heavenly Father, I declare that the joy that is in me—Your joy!—is greater than the circumstances that surround me. In times of adversity I draw strength from You. Keep the music coming! I will rejoice in You always. Hallelujah for the joy found in You, which is unspeakably rich in times of adversity. In Jesus' name; Amen.

FOR THE JOY

19

... looking unto Jesus, the author and finisher of our faith, who for the joy that was set before Him endured the cross, despising the shame, and has sat down at the right hand of the throne of God.

HEBREWS 12:2

The Apostle Paul possessed joy in the day of trouble. Paul was shipwrecked. Paul was stoned and left for dead. He was falsely imprisoned, cursed, and run out of town. After all that happened, he put his pen to parchment, and wrote: "Rejoice in the Lord always. Again I will say, rejoice!" (Philippians 4:4). Regardless of your circumstances, you can determine to rejoice and be glad; you can do it "for the joy."

Jesus endured the Cross, the Bible says, "for the joy that was set before Him." How in heaven's name can you have a joy, knowing that your body is about to be beaten to a bloody pulp; that you're going to be crowned with thorns; that nails and spikes are going to be driven by a sledge hammer through your feet and wrists; that spittle is going to drop off your beard when men spit in your face and mock you; that your side is about to be ripped open by a Roman spear? Where is the joy in that?

The joy of Jesus was in the fact that His suffering and death on the Cross was setting you and me free from the power of sin and Satan. That was His joy. It was His joy to lift you out of poverty and give you the riches of Abraham. It was His joy that opened the windows of heaven for you to receive more blessings than you can contain. With joy, He took your sickness and your suffering; and with great joy, He gave you divine health. With "the joy set before Him," He took your sins and shame and left them at the Cross, never to be remembered against you anymore. Stop talking about it and stop telling people about it. If God's forgotten it, you can forget it. If God's forgiven you, you can forgive you. Square your shoulders and embrace the redemption of the Cross. You are free from sin and shame forever.

Jesus rejoiced while headed to the Cross. Paul rejoiced while being shipwrecked, beaten, and imprisoned. Stephen rejoiced while being stoned as a martyr. The three Hebrew children rejoiced while being thrown into the fiery furnace. Joseph rejoiced despite being sold into slavery by his brothers. The father rejoiced when the prodigal son returned home. You, too, can rejoice—regardless of your circumstances—for the joy that is set before you.

PRAYER

In Jesus' name, I will rejoice, regardless of my circumstances, because of the joy that is set before me. That joy is a life free from sin and shame. I receive the healing power from sin and shame that You have given to me. Sin is never to be remembered against me anymore. Shame? What shame? I am free! Amen!

THE SHOUT OF JOY

20

Oh, clap your hands, all you peoples! Shout to God with the voice of triumph! For the LORD Most High is awesome; He is a great King over all the earth.

PSALM 47:1–2

There is a supernatural principle in the shout of joy. The shout of joy releases God's power to work in your life and on your behalf.

In Numbers 23:21, Balaam, a corrupt prophet, was hired by Balak to pronounce a curse on Israel, the children of God. When Balaam went out to pronounce the curse, he could not. He could only speak the words that God put in his mouth, which were blessings, not curses. Balaam returned to Balak saying, I cannot do it:

> *"God is not a man, that He should lie, nor a son of man, that He should repent. Has He said, and will He not do? Or has He spoken, and will He not make it good? Behold, I have received a command to bless; He has blessed, and I cannot reverse it. He has not observed iniquity in Jacob, nor has He seen wickedness in Israel. The LORD his God is with him, and the shout of a King is among them"* (Numbers 23:19–21).

Balaam could not curse the children of Israel because "the shout of a King is among them." The shout of joy protected God's chosen people by releasing God's power to work on their behalf. The purpose of the shout of joy, then, is to serve as a weapon of spiritual warfare.

> *Let the saints be joyful in glory; let them sing aloud on their beds. Let the high praises of God be in their mouth, and a two-edged sword in their hand, to execute vengeance on the nations, and punishments on the peoples; to*

bind their kings with chains, and their nobles with fetters of iron; to execute on them the written judgment—this honor have all His saints. Praise the LORD! (Psalm 149:5–8).

"Let the saints be joyful in glory ... Let the high praises of God [the shout] be in their mouth ... to bind their kings with chains ..." Your shout of praise to God releases Him to go to war against your enemies on your behalf.

Think about that. The next time you get in an old-fashioned, supernatural slug fest, lift your hands and say, "Lord, I'm just going to give You a shout of praise that my enemies are going to be destroyed, and this problem is going to be done, once and for all." When you do this, I want you to know that heaven is going to come down and glory will fill your soul. Hallelujah! Let God arise!

PRAYER

God, I come to You with a mighty shout, a mighty shout of joy and praise. I come in the power that Christ died and rose again to give me. Soon and very soon Jesus will descend from heaven with a shout, with the voice of an archangel, and with Your trumpet. Yes, and Amen!

THE WALLS OF JERICHO

21

So the people shouted when the priests blew the trumpets. And it happened when the people heard the sound of the trumpet, and the people shouted with a great shout, that the wall fell down flat. Then the people went up into the city, every man straight before him, and they took the city.

JOSHUA 6:20

Jericho represents "mission impossible." The walls of Jericho were considered a military impossibility to penetrate or to climb over. Jericho was an undefeatable foe. Jericho was the first city on the way to the Promised Land that the Israelites had to conquer in order to get the inheritance God had promised them for hundreds of years. Jericho was a barrier to what God had promised them and a barrier to their destiny.

So, God said, here's what I want you to do. I want you to walk around the walls, once a day for six days. And on the seventh day, the number of completion, I want you to walk around the walls seven times then blow the shofar, the ram's horn, and shout.

Joshua gathered all the people and gave them the Lord's instructions. He told them to walk around the walls, once a day for six straight days. And he told the people: "You shall not shout or make any noise with your voice, nor shall a word proceed out of your mouth, until the day I say to you, 'Shout!' Then you shall shout" (Joshua 6:10).

They walked in silence, around the walls of Jericho, once a day for six straight days. Then, on the seventh day, at the appointed time, the priests lifted the horns to their mouths, and they blew the mighty sound:

But it came to pass on the seventh day that they rose early, about the dawning of the day, and marched around the city seven times in the same manner. On that day only they marched around the city seven times. And the seventh time it happened, when the priests blew the trumpets, that Joshua said to the people: "Shout, for the LORD has given you the city!" (Joshua 6:15–16).

The people shouted—"a great shout"—when the priests blew the trumpets and "the wall fell down flat." The Israelites stormed Jericho and took the city that had stood in the way of their inheritance. The impossible happened. Invisible hands pushed that wall down. There was a supernatural victory that was implemented by shouting.

Many of you have walked around your problem for months, for years. You have allowed some "Jericho" to block you from your spiritual inheritance. You've allowed it to destroy your peace and happiness, maybe for an entire generation, and prevent you from obtaining the total victory that God has for you to live in. Friend, you have the spiritual license and the right, entreated by God, to shout it down! Give the walls of your "Jericho" a shout down! Ready? Shout!

PRAYER

God, I declare that it is time for the walls of my "Jericho" to come down! In Your strength and power, I will shout a mighty shout, for the weapons of my warfare are not carnal but mighty in You for pulling down strongholds. I shout it down! In Jesus' name; Amen.

THEN AND WHEN

22

When He had said this, He showed them His hands and His side. Then the disciples were glad when they saw the Lord.

JOHN 20:20

The secret of Christian joy hangs on two words: "then" and "when." John 20:20 says, "THEN the disciples were glad WHEN they saw the Lord." Then and when.

When you see the Lord, *then* you will be glad. *When* you see Him high and lifted up, *then* you will be glad. *When* disease attacks your body and you see Him as the Great Physician, *then* you will be glad. *When* you're burdened beyond bearing and you see Him as your burden bearer, *then* you will be glad. *When* you feel lonely and forsaken—and indeed you may be right now as you read this—you will see Him as the friend that sticks closer than a brother, saying "I am with you always, even to the ends of the age" (Matthew 28:20), *then* you will be glad. *When* you are in a financial crisis and you see Him as your source, as your *Jehovah Jireh*, as the "Lord Who Provides," *then* you will see the tree planted by the rivers of living water, whose leaf will not wither, and you will be glad.

It is far too easy for people to go about their daily lives and think that they are in control. But when you consider that God is the Creator of all things and He knows the number of hairs on your head (even if that number is zero!), and He knew you in your mother's womb before you even took your first breath of air, it is impossible not to see Him at work all around you. He is in the rising of the sun and the place that it sets. He is in the mundane and the miraculous. He is in the tree that withers and the one that bears fruit. He is with your prodigal child and the lost sheep of the world. He is with kings and queens and donkeys and is even in the belly of the whale. *When* you see His hand upon the earth and the stars in the sky and everything in between, *then* you will be glad.

What you see when you look at Jesus will determine if you are glad. Mary saw Him as a baby in Bethlehem's manger. The disciples saw Him as a great teacher, as a rabbi. The Pharisees thought of Him as a demonized heretic. Rome saw Him as an insurrectionist, too dangerous to live. But *when* we see Him as He is, the Bright and Morning Star, the King of all kings, the Lord of all lords, the Light of the World, the Lord of Glory, and our soon and coming King, *then* we can be glad. Hallelujah! Give God praise!

PRAYER

God, I believe all Your promises in Your Word are true. I know them to be true because I have seen them at work in my own life. You are who You say You are, and You do what You say You will do. You fulfill all Your promises. When I look back over my life and see the ways You have shown up and cared for me, then I am glad! In Jesus' name; Amen.

THE SEVEN WEAPONS OF SATAN

23

A merry heart does good, like medicine, but a broken spirit dries the bones.

PROVERBS 17:22

There are seven weapons that Satan uses to destroy the mind and the body: anxiety, fear, depression, resentment, insecurity, rejection, and discouragement. And they are all intended to steal your joy, sap your strength, and leave you bone tired.

Anxiety? Joy stealer. Fear? Joy stealer. Depression? Joy stealer. Resentment? Joy stealer. Insecurity? Joy stealer. Rejection? Joy stealer. Discouragement? Joy stealer.

Is Satan currently using one of these weapons against you? Are you paralyzed by fear, unable to overcome your feelings of resentment or rejection? Are you unable to take risks because of insecurity? Feeling discouraged or anxious about everything? Jesus has the antidote for you! You can fight back with the joy of the Lord.

When was the last time you had a good laugh? A deep-down belly laugh like when you were a kid? Laugh experts say that kids laugh an average of 400 times a day, but adults can only work up about 17 to 20 laughs a day. For some of you even 17 laughs a day might be a bit of a stretch! My mom used to say, "A day without laughter is like a day without sunshine." Gloom and doom!

Jesus said, "If a house is divided against itself, that house cannot stand" (Mark 3:25). Some of you are living in a divided house, saying things out of your mouth that do not line up with the Word of God. Is this you? Has your resentment destroyed your peace? Have you lost your joy? Has insecurity caused you to lose your zest for life? Has the rejection of your past destroyed your present? Is anxiety threatening to destroy your future? Are you discouraged or afraid? Recognize these symptoms for what they are—the weapons of Satan—and nip them in the bud with this simple equation: submit plus resist equals bye-bye Satan! "Therefore submit to God. Resist the devil and he will flee from you" (James 4:7).

Jesus also says, "The thief does not come except to steal, and to kill, and to destroy. I have come that they may have life, and that they may have it more abundantly" (John 10:10). If it is stealing your joy, killing your dreams, destroying your life, then it is 100 percent of the devil. But you can fight back with the joy of the Lord and with the Word. You can take back what the enemy has stolen.

> But those who wait on the LORD shall renew their strength; they shall mount up with wings like eagles, they shall run and not be weary, they shall walk and not faint (Isaiah 40:31).

Laugh at the devil right in his face for thinking he had any chance against you, child of God!

PRAYER

Heavenly Father, in the name of the Lord Jesus Christ, I cast all resentment and bitterness out of my life. I will fight back with joy. I will live in peace. The sound of laughter will fill my home again, because You are the joy of my soul. Amen and amen!

JOY IS A CHOICE

24

Therefore you now have sorrow; but I will see you again and your heart will rejoice, and your joy no one will take from you.

JOHN 16:22

Joy overcomes sorrow. I'm not talking about clinical depression, the medical condition. I'm talking about less than happy, the blues, the blahs. How many of you have that from time to time? Almost everyone has been less than happy at some point in their lives, and great spiritual men are no exception.

Consider Moses: After leading the children of Israel out of captivity, he went up Mount Sinai and spoke to the Lord, face-to-face. He had been gone for forty days, in the presence of God, and his face was aglow with *shekinah* glory. It was one of the most powerful, transformative experiences of his life. He was on cloud nine. However, when he came down off that mountain, he discovered that the children of God had come up with a new theology—the golden calf theology—and they were worshipping idols. Moses went from perfect peace to total devastation in a matter of seconds. He was so distraught that he threw down the Ten Commandments and broke them at the base of the mountain (see Exodus 32:19).

But Moses wasn't the only man of God to have a bad day. Job, too, was depressed. So depressed that he "cursed the day of his birth" (Job 3:1). Elijah also came down with a case of the blues, making him feel like he was the only one left who still believed in and followed God (see 1 Kings 19:10).

The blues aren't just limited to the great men of the Bible. Winston Churchill suffered from depression, which he described as a "black dog" that he couldn't get away from. Charles Haddon Spurgeon was preaching in his church in London, England, once when a mentally ill man screamed, "Fire! Fire!" Several people were trampled to death attempting to escape this false alarm. It literally broke the heart and mind of that great preacher. Despite being a man of God, he was not immune to feeling down. The deacons took Spurgeon to their home and prayed for him around the clock until his mind was healed. The peace of God restored him and after that his sermons were carried around the world.

The fact is, almost everyone gets the blues. But it is staying there that is the issue. Staying in the blahs of life is a decision, but so is choosing joy. Joy is a decision. It's a decision to discipline your thought life. It's a decision to abandon the whiny, self-piteous, thumb-sucking things you're going through that make you feel like Elijah—misunderstood and alone. It is a decision to give God total control of your life and trust that everything is going to be all right.

PRAYER

Lord, I declare that I have the right to choose joy. Take this sorrow from me and replace it with joy, a joy that no one can take from me. I give You control. Work all things together for my good. In Jesus' name; Amen.

THE ROYAL FAMILY

25

For you are all sons of God through faith in Christ Jesus. For as many of you as were baptized into Christ have put on Christ. There is neither Jew nor Greek, there is neither slave nor free, there is neither male nor female; for you are all one in Christ Jesus. And if you are Christ's, then you are Abraham's seed, and heirs according to the promise.

GALATIANS 3:26–29

The royal blood of heaven is flowing in your veins. Your faith in Christ Jesus makes you an heir according to the promise that God made with Abraham. As a child of God, you have authority. You are a threat to the prince of darkness. When you, as a redeemed, spirit-filled child of God roll over in bed, every demon trembles, because you are a blood-covered, royal child of the living God. And you have the power to crush the powers and principalities of darkness. You are the King's child!

Since the mid-80s, I have traveled regularly to Washington, D.C. In Washington, anyone who has direct access to the President of the United States has awesome power to achieve political objectives. People who have access to him get paid millions of dollars by corporations to represent them, because in a single day, the President can make their fortunes change dramatically for the good. So how does that involve you? You are a child of God. You have direct access to the Creator of heaven and earth. All you have to do is ask in the name of Jesus, and he will do it: "And whatever you ask in My name, that I will do, that the Father may be glorified in the Son" (John 14:13).

With great joy, Jesus of Nazareth has given you direct access. You don't have to make an appointment or wait in line. You simply call on the name that's above every name, and instantly, you're in the presence of the Creator of heaven and earth, the Conqueror of death, hell, and the grave, the Great Physician of every sickness. Rejoice and be exceedingly glad!

When James wrote his epistle to the twelve tribes, he began by saying: "My brethren, count it all joy when you fall into various trials" (James 1:2). By writing to "my brethren," James was calling every believer in the New Testament Church his relative. We are all related to each other! We are blood relatives because of the Cross.

"Rejoice in the Lord always ..." (Philippians 4:4). Say that out loud: "Rejoice in the Lord always." In the good times, in the bad times, start receiving the presence of the God in the room where you are. When you receive His name, you receive His authority. Claim it! Exercise it! Acknowledge the fact that through your faith in Christ Jesus, you are a blood-bought child of God!

PRAYER

Father God, I accept my position as Your beloved child and heir to the promise. I receive the authority to call on Your name and know that You will answer me. I give thanks in all things, because I belong to the Royal Family! We are blood! You are my Kinsman Redeemer! In Jesus' name; Amen.

THE SEARCH FOR PEACE

26

Therefore, having been justified by faith, we have peace with God through our Lord Jesus Christ.

ROMANS 5:1

The search for peace has become an international obsession. We're living in an age of anxiety, saturated with fear and uncertainty, turmoil, trouble, wars, rumors of wars, and betrayal. This nation is more divided now than at any time since the Civil War. Americans are pleading for peace. The legions of this tormented earth are begging for peace. We have peace marches. We have a Peace Corps. We have peace conferences. But there is no peace. We write books about peace of mind and they sell like hot cakes. Why? Because we're looking for in a book, what we don't have in our lives.

Everything we do is designed to produce peace. The U.S. Army, Navy, Marine Corps, and Air Force exist to produce peace where there is no peace. Every police officer has one goal: to protect and defend the peace and make it possible for the citizens of their city to live in peace. And yet, we continue to come up short.

Is peace a lost cause? No! Peace is available, but we have been searching for it in all the wrong places and trying to create it with human constructs. Peace, lasting peace, is available but only through Jesus Christ, the Prince of Peace.

Luke 2:14 says, "Glory to God in the highest, and on earth peace, goodwill toward men!" Angels sang that on the first Christmas morning, at the birth of the Prince of Peace. That latter phrase, "goodwill toward men," is misleading in English. The Revised Standard Version says, "Glory to God in the highest, and on earth peace among men with whom he is pleased!" The original Greek reads, "Peace on earth to those of whom God approves." Peace on earth is possible, but only with God's approval.

> But the wicked are like the troubled sea, when it cannot rest, whose waters cast up mire and dirt. "There is no peace," says my God, "for the wicked" (Isaiah 57:20–21).

There is no peace for the wicked. None. The idea of universal peace for a Christ-rejecting, God-hating, pleasure-loving world enslaved by materialism and socialism is a pipe dream. Peace is the gift of God, and He gives it only to those who bow their knee to Jesus Christ as Lord and Savior.

Still searching for peace? Search for Jesus and you will find peace.

PRAYER

Father, I declare that there is only one way to have peace in this nation, in our lives, in our world, and that is through total surrender to Your Son, Jesus Christ. I bow my knee to the Prince of Peace and receive the joy of peace available to the children of God. In Jesus' name; Amen.

BE AT PEACE

27

If it is possible, as much as depends on you, live peaceably with all men.

ROMANS 12:18

What is peace? If you are looking for something and you can't define it, you are in trouble because you'll never know when it arrives.

Let me tell you what peace is not. Peace is not placidity. Peace is not having low blood pressure. Peace is not sitting around unconcerned about everything. Peace is not stoic silence. How many of you know that you can be silent on the outside and boiling on the inside? How many of you have that gift? That is not peace! Peace is not cowering before intimidation. Some people appear to be at peace because they are afraid of conflict. Peace is not the absence of tension. Peace is not tranquility. Peace is not the blue haven of the untroubled life. In this life, there is no such thing as total absence of tension. To pray for peace, if you are looking for a life free of risk and responsibility, is to pray for the peace of death.

Until then, get ready to accept your share of the responsibility, to take your share of the risks, to be hurt, to be offended. Get over it. Grow up and produce something!

The Bible says in Romans 12:18, "If possible, so far as it depends on you, be at peace with all men" (NASB). You hear that verse all the time: "be at peace with all men." But that is leaving out half the verse! The verse says, "If possible ... be at peace with all men." *If possible.* Sometimes it is not possible! But if it is possible, be at peace.

I once heard a story about a Quaker, whose faith prohibited any type of violence. He was awakened by two thieves breaking into his house, so he got his twelve-gauge shotgun off the shelf. He turned and faced the men and said, "Brothers, peace be unto you. I want you to know that I have no intention of harming you, but you are standing where I'm about to shoot."

"*If possible* ... be at peace with all men." If not, look out!

PRAYER

Lord, I declare that in all situations where there is a possibility of peace, if there is any way that I can create peace in my life, relationships, work, and home through Your loving and gracious hand, then I will be at peace with everyone! In Jesus' name; Amen.

SURRENDER

28

Cast your burden on the LORD, and He shall sustain you; He shall never permit the righteous to be moved.

PSALM 55:22

John 8:32 says, "And you shall know the truth, and the truth shall make you free." What is the truth that will set you free? The truth is, you can't do it on your own. You are not the Master of the Universe, and you will never have peace in your life if you try to be. Once you come to accept that truth, you can have peace.

Are you a Christian, but don't have peace? Do you want the peace of God? Maybe it's in your marriage, or with your family. Maybe it's a business matter or maybe things have just gotten out of control. Sometimes problems can be so large that the very magnitude of them drives peace from you. I want you to listen to me: I have been in ministry for 60 years, and there have been times that problems were so massive it was all I could do to wrap my brain around them. I'd just sit down and pray, "Lord, I'm resigning today as the General Manager of the Universe. You take this job. You carry this burden. I don't even know where to pick it up." And suddenly the Lord would move in and the answer would come.

First Peter 5:7 says, "casting all your care upon Him, for He cares for you." God cares about you enough to carry your burdens. In fact, He wants you to "cast" them upon Him. Whenever the Bible talks about casting something, it means you are to throw it off, throw it out, throw it away. Hebrews 12:1 says, "... let us throw off everything that hinders and the sin that so easily entangles ..." (NIV). Throw your burdens, your sins, your cares on God and trust Him to take care of them!

If you don't have peace in your life, it could be because you have never surrendered to the Lordship of Jesus Christ. When you turn it over to the Lord, things will begin to happen supernaturally that you just couldn't imagine ever happening. Chains will be broken. Addictions will no longer have their hold on you. Relationships will be restored. Doors will be opened that seemed permanently shut. Life will be better than you ever imagined possible.

> ... *"Most assuredly, I say to you, whoever commits sin is a slave of sin. And a slave does not abide in the house forever, but a son abides forever. Therefore if the Son makes you free, you shall be free indeed"* (John 8:34–36).

You can be free and have peace when you cast your cares on the Lord and surrender to His care. So, go ahead: lift your hands and give it to the Lord!

PRAYER

Lord, I surrender. I cast my cares on You and know that You will sustain me because You care for me. Forgive me for trying to do it on my own. The weight has been lifted. The burden is no longer mine. I am free! In Jesus' name; Amen.

GLORY DAYS

29

"Do not remember the former things, nor consider the things of old. Behold, I will do a new thing, now it shall spring forth; shall you not know it? I will even make a road in the wilderness and rivers in the desert."

ISAIAH 43:18–19

Many people are totally controlled by what has happened to them in the past. They fear that they will never be as good at something as they were in the past, or that because they were so bad they will never be able to move forward. But whether your past was awful or "the glory days," you must move pass your past!

Were you the salesman of the year last year? Forget it. Was there a pink slip waiting in your office mailbox six months ago? Forget it. Did you win the state championship in high school? Forget it. Were you always the last one picked in gym class? Forget it. The energy you had that was so wonderful when you started your first real job—it won't pay the light bill tomorrow. Forget it, forget it, forget it. Get up and get on your bicycle and start pumping. Move beyond your achievements. Move beyond your failures and setbacks. Move to the love of God. Move on to the joy, peace, and hope that God has for you. Get moving!

The Bible is full of men and women who had to get pass their past in order to achieve God's plan for their lives. Moses was ran out of Pharaoh's house after he killed an Egyptian but returned to rescue the Israelites out of slavery. David had an affair with Uriah's wife, but went on to father Solomon, the wisest man who ever lived. Naomi's husband and both of her sons died, but through her daughter-in-law Ruth, she was able to have a family again. Saul persecuted Christians, but after his conversion experience became the man famously remembered as the Apostle Paul. Peter denied Jesus three times but went on to be the rock upon which the Church was built. Each of these men and women were able to move pass their past so that God could use their future for His glory.

Your past does not control your potential. You need to have the daring to see yourself as God sees you, as someone who lives without limitations. Matthew 17:20 says, "nothing will be impossible for you" if you have faith in Him. There is nothing you cannot overcome. There is no reason your days can't be, today and every day, moving forward. There is nothing to stop you from the plans and purposes that God has for your life. There is nothing you cannot do. Nothing!

Nothing is impossible with God! Don't allow your past to control your future. Get up! Get moving! Dust yourself off! Dream the impossible dream. Dare to be yourself in the face of adversity.

PRAYER

God, I know that the past is not the path to peace. My past is nothing compared to what You want for my future. You are doing something new; I can already feel it! And I am moving forward to lay hold of it. Nothing is impossible with You! In Jesus' name; Amen.

GOD IS NOT A PEACEMAKER

30

"Do not think that I came to bring peace on earth. I did not come to bring peace but a sword."

MATTHEW 10:34

In Deuteronomy 20, God told Israel: When you pass through a new land en route to the Promised Land, ask the people of that land for peace. Pay for the water that you use. Pay for grazing rights for your livestock. Pay for everything. But if they will not be at peace with you, then attack. Destroy them and make them your slaves.

Whoa! Did you know that was in the Bible? God is clearly not a peacemaker!

King David said, "Blessed be the LORD my Rock, who trains my hands for war, and my fingers for battle" (Psalm 144:1). The Lord has taught my hands to war. That's in your Bible. God is not a pacifist!

Neither was His Son Jesus Christ. Look at Jesus. He invades the temple with a whip in His hand. His eyes are blazing in rage as He looks at the people and says, "'My house shall be called a house of prayer,' but you have made it a 'den of thieves'" (Matthew 21:13). Jesus turned the tables loaded with money over. He stampeded the sheep. He let the turtledoves escape. The terrified money changers tucked tail and ran. Jesus was cleaning out the Wall Street of His day. He was like a lion charging out of a thicket. Why? Because He was the Living God, and truth was all He would accept.

Let me shock you with this: it was never God's plan for there to be universal peace.

Matthew 10:34 says that Jesus didn't come to bring peace, but a sword. A sword divides. And the world is divided over Jesus alone. You either accept Him or reject Him. You are either in the kingdom of light or the kingdom of darkness. You're not kind of in one and kind of in the other. You are either in or you're not. You are either a servant to Jesus Christ or a slave to sin and Satan. That's the Word of God.

Jesus was a warrior who went to the Cross and fought the most vicious battle in the history of humanity. He fought for your soul and mine. He bled. He died for our redemption. He is our King! He is our Lord! He is coming again with power and great glory. He is victorious over the world, the flesh, and the devil. And He didn't become victorious by begging the devil to back up. He kicked him off planet earth! Hallelujah to the Lamb of God!

PRAYER

God in heaven, I come to You today knowing that my peace was purchased through the violence and the blood of the Cross of Christ. Jesus, by His action, taught that it is sinful to be at peace with iniquity. The world is divided by the sword and I side with Jesus—100 percent, I am all in! In Jesus' name; Amen.

PEACE IS NOT THE END GOAL

31

But the fruit of the Spirit is love, joy, peace, longsuffering, kindness, goodness, faithfulness, gentleness, self-control. Against such there is no law.

GALATIANS 5:22–23

Where is peace to be found? What I'm about to tell you, you've probably never heard before. It can change your life forever. Are you ready? Nowhere in the Bible is peace sought as the "end goal" of existence. I repeat: peace is not the end goal!

In the Bible, peace is a consequence, not the goal; it's the result, not the reason.

Galatians 5:22 says, "The fruit of the Spirit is love, joy, peace, longsuffering, kindness, goodness, faithfulness." Peace is the *fruit* of the Spirit, not the Spirit itself. Peace is a by-product of the Spirit of God in you.

Peace is the *fruit* of reconciliation, the rightness of heart, which comes through forgiveness.

> *Let the wicked forsake his way, and the unrighteous man his thoughts; let him return to the LORD, and He will have mercy on him; and to our God, for He will abundantly pardon* (Isaiah 55:7).

Peace is the *fruit* of responsibility—of facing life, not fleeing from it. Peace is not detachment from risk and responsibility. The Bible is not a book for people sitting on the sidelines of life watching the world go by. There are giants to fight! There are battles to win! Jesus said, "take up your cross and follow me."

Then Jesus said to his disciples, "Whoever wants to be my disciple must deny themselves and take up their cross and follow me" (Matthew 16:24 NIV).

A cross is a burden to bear. It's a mission to accomplish. Every person reading this has a divine assignment. And there are going to be risks and responsibilities in making that assignment happen. It's not designed to keep you placid and uncommitted. Christianity is peace in conflict, peace in the storm, peace!

Forgiveness, responsibility, and wisdom are all freely given through the Holy Spirit to those who seek after God. James says, "you should ask God, who gives generously to all without finding fault, and it will be given to you" (1:5 NIV). We serve a generous God. Need wisdom? Ask God to guide you through the Holy Spirit at work in your life. Need forgiveness? Repent of your sins, ask for forgiveness and receive it. Want purpose? Ask God for the strength and tenacity to face your responsibilities head on, to bear your cross, and to walk out your divine assignment. With wisdom, God will give you peace. With responsibility, God will give you peace. With forgiveness, God will give you peace.

True peace will come when you stop searching for peace as the end goal, and instead start seeking God. Start taking responsibility for your life; start asking forgiveness for your sins and follow Him.

PRAYER

Lord Jesus, I receive Your peace, which You freely give to me as a by-product of Your Spirit in my life. Thank You for forgiveness. Thank You for wisdom. Thank You for my divine assignment. Amen and amen.

GUILT IS REAL; GUILT IS A GIFT

32

Peace I leave with you, My peace I give to you; not as the world gives do I give to you. Let not your heart be troubled, neither let it be afraid.

JOHN 14:27

In every man's heart there lurks and lives—whether he lives in a mansion or a mud hut—a sense of conscience and a hunger for righteousness. Because we all have a conscience and want to do what is right, there are consequences when we do wrong. Among those consequences are feelings of guilt and a lack of peace.

Our generation is now dismissing the whole idea of guilt, responsibility, and that we even need God's forgiveness. Please understand: that's not biblical!

Uneasiness in the heart comes from a sense of guilt. That sense of guilt is God-given. It's a cop that follows us everywhere we go. Guilt is real. The pain of our conscience is real. It will not shut up. We cannot sweep it under the bed. We cannot drown our conscience at the seashore. We cannot drown it with drugs or debauchery or drunkenness. We have created devices to make us feel good without being good. There are pills and needles to mask pain, to make us feel good for a moment. But sooner or later, we're going to get sober enough to see ourself in the mirror. And when we get there, the thundering echo of God's cop, our conscience, is going to scream: you did wrong!

Have you been looking for peace in all the wrong places? People of all ages are searching for peace in marijuana, cocaine, heroin, sex, relationships, money, material things, the list goes on and on. But do any of them have peace? No! They have no peace. They are empty, confused. They are ships without rudders, surrendered to the wrong power.

Sooner or later, because you know the Scriptures, it will dawn on you that as soon as you repent and confess your sin, God will forgive you, remove your guilt, and you will feel the joy of the Lord that "maketh rich and addeth no sorrow" (Proverbs 10:22). Do you know how anxious God is to forgive you? His Son went to the Cross and with joy took all the sins in your life and washed them with His precious blood. But you have to ask for that forgiveness.

Let me tell you this: lots of things can make you sing but they won't set you free. When you surrender to the Lord Jesus Christ, then you can sing with pure joy. It will break the oppression that's following you. It will bring peace that surpasses all understanding. If you want joy, real joy, real peace, wonderful peace, you must repent of your sins, receive His forgiveness, and surrender to the Lordship of Jesus Christ.

PRAYER

Heavenly Father, in the name of the Lord Jesus Christ, the Prince of Peace, I receive the peace that surpasses understanding. Father, You know the burden that I'm carrying. I place it in Your hands. I pledge and promise to live a righteous life according to Your Word. I know that peace will come as I confess and forsake all my sin. In Jesus' name, I receive Your peace; Amen!

THE ADJUSTMENT GOSPEL

33

He who covers his sins will not prosper, but whoever confesses and forsakes them will have mercy.

PROVERBS 28:13

Adjustment is the new gospel in America. The Adjustment Gospel says:

> Adjust to your sin. Accept your sins. For heaven's sake, don't rise above your sin; get used to it. Everybody's doing it. That's just the way you are. You can't change. Your mother and your father were like that. God loves you just as you are.

That's what the world is teaching. Even some universities and churches are teaching that message. Far too many people are hearing messages like that today; but I assure you—that is not God's message!

Proverbs 28:13 says, "... whoever confesses and forsakes them [his sins] will have mercy." You need to hear that condition: whoever confesses AND forsakes his sin. You can confess your sin every Friday night and still miss out on God's mercy. Until you confess and *forsake* your sins, you haven't walked away from them. To *forsake* means just that—to turn away, to leave them behind, to give them up.

When the Pharisees brought Jesus a woman caught in adultery, Jesus said, "He who is without sin among you, let him throw a stone at her first" (John 8:7). Everyone walked away. Jesus, though He truly was without sin, said He also did not condemn her. In fact, He forgave her; but He also asked her to forsake her sin: "... go and sin no more" (v. 11). That's what it means to forsake sin. That is what Jesus asks of us. To give up that which separates us from Him.

Don't let a religious exercise fool you into the idea that you have a ticket to heaven because you've confessed something. Until you forsake your sin, you're not with the Lord. The Adjustment Gospel drives us to clinics, not churches. It makes us masters at creating alibis for our sin. But God's Word couldn't be any clearer: "He who covers his sins will not prosper ..."

Listen to this. Rationalizing sin is inherent with the Adamic Nature. When God came looking for Adam and Eve in the Garden, He asked Adam: "Have you eaten from the tree of which I commanded you that you should not eat?" (Genesis 3:11). Adam looked at God and said, "The woman whom You gave to be with me, she gave me of the tree, and I ate" (v. 12). So, God asked Eve: "What is this you have done?" And she said, "The serpent deceived me, and I ate" (v. 13). Adam blamed God and Eve; Eve blamed the serpent; but neither took any responsibility. Both Adam and Eve rationalized what they did. When you rationalize your sin, you're deceiving yourself at the expense of your eternal soul. You must confess and forsake your sin or your sin is still with you.

PRAYER

God, I confess my sin and forsake it. I will not adjust to it. I am turning my back on sin and turning my face toward You. I am not perfect; I will sin again. But when I do, I will confess again and forsake again and not make excuses. I receive Your mercy. Thank You for Your grace! In Jesus' name; Amen.

FIRST COMES RIGHTEOUSNESS, THEN COMES PEACE

34

*... if My people
who are called
by My name
will humble
themselves, and
pray and seek
My face, and
turn from their
wicked ways,
then I will hear
from heaven,
and will forgive
their sin and
heal their land.*

2 CHRONICLES 7:14

Will there ever be universal peace on earth? Not until there's universal repentance of sin on earth. Armies and peace treaties, bullets, bombs, tanks, and planes—they will determine who kills who first. But universal peace is not going to come until there's a righteous revolution when we, as a people, decide that we're going to live by God's law and accept Jesus Christ as Lord and Savior.

King David said in Psalm 85:10, "Mercy and truth have met together; righteousness and peace have kissed." Notice the sequence. What comes first, peace or righteousness? Righteousness! Righteousness comes *before* the peace of God. In the book of Hebrews, Christ is proclaimed first as the "King of Righteousness," and later in the same verse, the "King of Peace": "to whom also Abraham gave a tenth part of all, first being translated 'king of righteousness,' and then also king of Salem, meaning 'king of peace'" (Hebrews 7:2). Righteousness, then peace. Paul wrote to the Romans: "for the kingdom of God is not eating and drinking, but righteousness and peace and joy in the Holy Spirit" (Romans 14:17). What comes before peace and joy? Righteousness.

What God shows us in the Bible is not just good advice, it is God's revelation to man. Peace on earth is simple: seek righteousness, then peace will come. Our frustration occurs when we reverse the order. We want peace without righteousness. We want the gifts of God without the rule of God. Everyone wants peace, but they want it their way. Note: it's much easier to hate war than to hate the attitude and sin within us that make war possible.

The price for world peace is world righteousness, a righteous revolution. And it starts with you, the individual. In this age, we need to heed the advice of Jesus, who said: "But seek first the kingdom of God and His righteousness, and all these things shall be added to you" (Matthew 6:33). Righteousness first, then ALL these things shall be added unto you: peace, prosperity, blessing, joy, hope. It'll all come your way as soon as you are righteous in the eyes of God.

Do you want peace? Real peace? Lasting peace? Seek righteousness and peace will come.

PRAYER

Lord, I surrender to Your will as Lord of my life. May Your peace be my portion today and every day for the rest of my life. This is the covenant You have made with me, that if I follow You in righteousness, then joy—real joy, lasting joy—will be mine for all eternity. In Jesus' name, I receive this joy today. Amen.

THE RECIPE FOR PEACE

35

"Blessed is the man to whom the LORD shall not impute sin."

ROMANS 4:8

There is a beautiful scene in the Bible that portrays a woman washing Jesus' feet with her hair. Jesus is at the table with Simon the Leper, preparing to eat. An unnamed woman, known only as a sinful woman in Luke's depiction (see Luke 7:36–50), is in the house and she has brought an alabaster flask of oil. The woman washes Jesus' feet with her tears and her hair, then proceeds to anoint them with the fragrant oil. Of course, Simon is aghast, thinking Jesus can't surely be a prophet or He would know what kind of woman this is who is touching His feet. As Jesus was fond of doing, He told Simon a parable:

> *"There was a certain creditor who had two debtors. One owed five hundred denarii, and the other fifty. And when they had nothing with which to repay, he freely forgave them both. Tell Me, therefore, which of them will love him more?" Simon answered and said, "I suppose the one whom he forgave more." And He said to him, "You have rightly judged"* (Luke 7:41–43).

Jesus concludes the parable by comparing Simon to the debtor who owed 50 denarii, and the sinful woman with the alabaster flask to the debtor who owed 500.

> *... "Do you see this woman? I entered your house; you gave Me no water for My feet, but she has washed My feet with her tears and wiped them with the hair of her head. You gave Me no kiss, but this woman has not ceased to kiss My feet since the time I came in. You did not anoint My head with*

oil, but this woman has anointed My feet with fragrant oil. Therefore I say to you, her sins, which are many, are forgiven, for she loved much. But to whom little is forgiven, the same loves little" (vv. 44–47).

The creditor in the parable forgave both debtors—both the debtor who owed 500 denarii and the debtor who owed only 50. Jesus implies that He has forgiven both the sinful woman and Simon the Leper. Of the sinful woman, Jesus says, "her sins, which are many, are forgiven." He says this is obvious by how much she loves Him. Jesus indicates that Simon doesn't love Him nearly as much, even though he, too, was forgiven of sins.

Jesus closes out this scene by telling the woman: "Your sins are forgiven. ... Your faith has saved you. Go in peace" (vv. 48, 50). Forgiveness and faith are the recipe for peace!

In the Upper Room, the night before the Cross, the night before Gethsemane, the night before the sins of the world were going to be cast upon Him, Jesus said to His disciples, "Peace I leave with you, My peace I give to you; not as the world gives do I give to you. Let not your heart be troubled, neither let it be afraid" (John 14:27). My friend, that's the kind of peace we are all looking for: the peace of God that surpasses all understanding, the peace of God that comes through forgiveness and faith. Blessed are those whose sin is forgiven, because they can walk in peace!

PRAYER

Jesus, I receive Your forgiveness of my many, many sins, in faith believing that You took them to the Cross and buried them there, never to be remembered any more. Through Your forgiveness, I have the peace that passes understanding, peace regardless of my circumstances, peace that can never be taken away! In Your name; Amen.

PURPOSE IN THE STORM

36

When you pass through the waters, I will be with you; and through the rivers, they shall not overflow you. When you walk through fire, you shall not be burned, nor shall the flame scorch you.

ISAIAH 43:2

Life is not a parade. It is a continuous series of storms. Those storms shake us, shape us, and inspire us to hold to the unchanging hand of God. When everything else is crumbling around us in the darkest hour of life, God does not fail us. God uses storms to teach us that we need Him every day and every hour of our lives.

God teaches us, through those storms, that He is all powerful, mighty, and that He alone is in control of planet Earth. Just about the time humanity begins to feel invincible, He demonstrates His absolute control of the world and our lives by the storms He sends and the storms He conquers. God uses storms to shake us out of our comfort zone into a position of complete surrender to Him for our survival. If we never had problems, how would we know that God could solve them? Truly, it is amazing what our God can do.

In 60 years of ministry, I have listened to stories of heartache, betrayal, honest confession of intentional sin, recklessness, and foolish choices. I have listened to sobbing voices express the fear of tomorrow, the bitterness that's in their heart, the rejection, unforgiveness, rage, regret, abandonment, lack of self-confidence, and insecurity they have experienced due to failure. All of these are storms. You may be going through a storm right now. It could be a make-or-break kind of storm.

Remember that the God we serve is the Master of the wind and waves. He is the Chain Breaker and the Way Maker. He is "the Way, the Truth, and the Life" (John 14:6). It is His voice that penetrates the darkness. He is still the Light of the World. He is still the Light of glory. He is still the Lion of Judah. He is still our companion in the valley of the shadow of death. He is our hope. He is our fortress. He is our high tower. He is the mighty God, the everlasting Father, and the Prince of Peace. He is the sea walker and the blind man healer. He is the champion of death, hell, and the grave. His name is Jesus, the Son of the Living God, heaven's hope, and hell's dread. Give Him praise!

PRAYER

Lord God, I recite the words of Psalm 121 as my faith declaration this day: I lift up my eyes to the hills – from whence does my help come? My help comes from You, who made heaven and earth. You will keep me from all evil; You shall preserve my soul. You will keep my going out and my coming in from this time forth, and even forevermore. In Jesus' name; Amen!

THE STORM OF FAILURE

37

For a righteous man may fall seven times and rise again, but the wicked shall fall by calamity.

PROVERBS 24:16

Who is there among us who has not failed? I have failed. You have failed. We have all tasted the bitter dregs of failure. Every day you see people captured and crushed by some personal failure. There's the college student who was dreaming of becoming a doctor but failed a course in comparative anatomy. There are endless numbers of people who walked into a dark storm that never ended. There's the man or woman captured in the storm of a broken home. The marriage that began with so much hope, with so much joy, with so much delight, is now a dark fight. It's a war zone. Life has become an endless bitter trail. There are thousands of Christians who make a glorious start at the Christian life; you know they are going to get to heaven if they don't run past it, but somewhere along the way, they got capsized by a wave, by a wind of adversity. Temptation took them over. Discouragement smashed them against the beach. They failed; and rather than get up, they gave up. They quit trying. Is this you?

I had a dear friend who was in a personal storm of moral failure. I told him of a loving God who was ready to forgive him and to give him a new beginning. He wasn't defensive or belligerent, but he wouldn't budge from his personal storm. For years, he lived in that storm, a total captive. He rejected the freedom that is possible through the Cross. Why? Because he would not admit that he failed. Is that you? Hear this: the greatest tragedy in life isn't to fall down, it is to stay down.

Proverbs 24:16 says, even a righteous man

falls, in fact he may fall seven times, yet he always gets back on his feet, he always rises again. If you have fallen, get up; Christ has conquered your storm. Start living again. Start loving again. Start believing again. Start achieving again. Listen to the voice of the Master. Your storm is over when you repent of your sins and receive His forgiveness: "... Though your sins are like scarlet, they shall be as white as snow; though they are red like crimson, they shall be as wool" (Isaiah 1:18). You are washed clean.

Are you like the prodigal son, sitting in some hog pen in the far country trying to be satisfied with the husk of a second-rate life, knowing full well that you have a father who wants to welcome you home? Stop it. In Jesus' name, GET UP! Get up, dust yourself off, and go back to your Father's house. There's repentance and mercy at your Father's house. At your Father's house is a new beginning. To *repent* means simply to turn around. So, turn around. Once you start heading in the right direction, I guarantee the Father will start running to meet you and welcome you home.

PRAYER

God, You are my Father in heaven, hallowed be Thy name. I choose this day to repent of my sins, to turn back to You. No matter how many times I may fall, I choose to get back up again. I choose to keep coming back to You. Thank You for welcoming me home! In Jesus' name; Amen.

A GREAT HISTORY OF FAILURE

38

Do not rejoice over me, my enemy; when I fall, I will arise; when I sit in darkness, the LORD will be a light to me.

MICAH 7:8

Conquering the storm of failure is the key to your success. You must be prepared to fail before you will ever succeed.

Did you know that George Washington's gifts of leadership and his willingness to sacrifice to accomplish the American dream were born out of failure? In 1754, as a young major in the Virginia militia, Washington was ordered to lead 350 royal recruits through the wilderness to the French-occupied Fort Duquesne (present-day Pittsburgh). Washington advanced on the enemy, he and his troops finding themselves up against 700 French soldiers and their Indian allies. In nine short hours, 30 of Washington's men were dead, seven were wounded, and many more had deserted. The battle was over. Washington had been defeated by a strategy he had never seen before: guerrilla warfare. The French and Indians had hidden behind rocks and trees, firing over the walls of the fort, wiping out Washington's men. Washington was forced to hand over his sword and sign a hastily-drafted article of surrender by candlelight in a driving hailstorm. George Washington, the future father of our country, lost his first battle and looked like a royal failure. It was a humiliating defeat. However, years later, when the British army—the best trained and equipped army in the world—landed on the shores of America, Washington remembered the tactics of the French and Indians. He put his men behind trees and rocks, routing and humiliating the British forces until he won. The point? Washington's total victory was made possible only by his total failure. Failure is a great teacher!

Washington wasn't the only president whose success was made possible by failure. Abraham Lincoln's long political career was a dreary series of failures. His first political effort for state legislator in Illinois failed in defeat; failure one. He tried his hand at business and failed; failure two. He was elected to Congress in 1846 but was defeated in re-election; failure three. He tried unsuccessfully to get an appointment with the U.S. Land Office; failure four. In 1856, he was beaten out as a candidate for Vice President; failure five. Two years later, he lost again to Stephen Douglas; failure six. Then in 1860, he was elected President of the United States. You can visit the Lincoln Memorial in Washington, D.C., where thousands of others gather to look at the brooding genius who crushed slavery, who held America together in its darkest hour, who endured more hatred than any other president. He changed the world because he had the strength to endure failure. He refused to surrender to the storms that plagued his life. He moved past the ridicule, the defeats, and the blame that was heaped upon him by Congress. History now calls him one of the greatest presidents in the history of America, despite his many failures.

I don't think it is a stretch to say that every person in American history went through a furnace of adversity to achieve greatness. Because if you cannot stand the fires of adversity and failure, you cannot stand the pressures of success.

PRAYER

Lord, I admit my failures, but I refuse to be bound by them. I will keep getting up. I will keep trying again. I believe that You will use my defeat as a stairway to my divine destiny. In Jesus' name; Amen.

THE ART OF FORGETTING

39

*Brethren, I do
not count myself
to have appre-
hended; but
one thing I do,
forgetting those
things which
are behind
and reaching
forward to those
things which are
ahead.*

PHILIPPIANS 3:13

During his childhood, Sir Walter Scott, who went on to be a successful poet, historian, and novelist, was called a dunce. As a youth, Napoleon Bonaparte, who later became emperor of France, was sent to military school. Einstein, a name now synonymous with genius, was told by his teachers that he was too dumb to learn. At the age of fifteen, Sir Isaac Newton, now considered one of the most influential scientists of all time, showed so little progress in school that his parents unenrolled him and put him to work on the farm.

What each of these men had in common was an ability to master the art of forgetting, letting go of the things of the past to achieve God's big dreams for their futures. As the Apostle Paul says, "forgetting those things which are behind and reaching forward to those things which are ahead" (Philippians 3:13). Forget the resentment. Forget your anxiety. Forget your past. Forget your rejection. Forget your disgust. Forget your frustration. Forget your anger. Forget the labels that others have put on you. Forget, and move on!

One man in the Bible who you would think would have a hard time forgetting is Joseph. Joseph was resented by his older brothers because he was his father's favorite son. Joseph had big dreams, but his brothers didn't want to hear it. They threw him into a pit, then later sold him into slavery. Despite their actions, Joseph continued to be a dreamer, and his dreams earned him a place in Pharaoh's household. Pharaoh gave Joseph a wife and they began to have children:

Joseph called the name of the first-born Manasseh: "For God has made me forget all my toil and all my father's house." And the name of the second he called Ephraim: "For God has caused me to be fruitful in the land of my affliction" (Genesis 41:51–52).

Names were incredibly important in biblical times. The names that Joseph gave his children showed that he had mastered the art of forgetting his brothers' opinions of him, which allowed him to move forward and receive God's blessing.

Are you allowing the opinions of others to frame your life? Master the art of forgetting! Stop allowing your past to control your future. Don't let anyone ever box you into their small dreams for your life. Live your life to the maximum every day that the sun comes up. Don't be ambushed by your problems, be led by your dreams. Let God Almighty guide you through the storm. Let Him build the foundation of your life. Let Him set you on fire with a burning vision and a hope that will not go away. I assure you, you will accomplish great things because God's blessing is greater than all the approval the world could ever give. God is your Father. Nothing is impossible to you. When you believe that, you'll never be the same.

PRAYER

Heavenly Father, I come before Your holy throne in the name of the Lord Jesus Christ. And I ask You, Father, to help me get pass the past. Lord Jesus Christ, let my hopes and dreams be reborn. Let me sing a song of joy again. Let this midnight of suffering and endless pain be over forever. In Jesus' name, I receive it today. Amen.

A PORTRAIT OF SUCCESS

40

"Behold, we are going up to Jerusalem, and the Son of Man will be betrayed to the chief priests and to the scribes; and they will condemn Him to death and deliver Him to the Gentiles; and they will mock Him, and scourge Him, and spit on Him, and kill Him. And the third day He will rise again."

MARK 10:33–34

Consider the storms of the greatest life ever lived. He was born in an obscure village. He was the child of a peasant woman. He grew up in another obscure village not far away. There He worked in a carpenter's shop until He was thirty years of age. He never wrote a book. He never held a public office. He didn't go to college. He never visited a large city. He never traveled more than 200 miles from the place of His birth. He did none of these things that are usually attributed to what is required for greatness. He had no credentials but Himself.

And then He turned 33 and found out who His real friends were. One doubted Him. One denied Him. Another sold Him for the price of a slave. They all scattered. He was nailed to a Roman cross between two thieves while dying. His executioners gambled for His robe. It was the only property He had on earth. When He was dead, He was laid in a borrowed grave through the pity of the one friend He had left. He was the portrait of failure.

Then came the third day. The Son of God walked out of that grave, the victor of death, hell, and the grave. The Champion of the Cross came out and declared the world to be free from the power of sin and Satan. When He rose, He signified the fact that we have eternal life. He was the Champion of Calvary! He is the Champion of the World, the Son of the living God. There is no other. Jesus is His name! God used the moment that Christ looked like a total failure to give us the greatest victory we have ever received.

Twenty centuries have come and gone. Today, Jesus of Nazareth is still the central figure of the human race and the leader of mankind's progress. Of all the armies that have ever marched, all the ships that have ever sailed, all the parliaments that have ever met, all the kings, queens, prime ministers, and presidents who have ever reigned, none have affected the lives of mankind on earth like that one singular life who refused to give in to the failure with which He was shrouded until the day He rose from the grave.

PRAYER

Jesus of Nazareth, You, more than any other, show me what it is to live a successful life. I will not live as the world tells me to live. I will walk in obedience to You and, despite all opposition, follow Your statutes from this day forward. You are the portrait of success. In Your name I pray; Amen.

GREAT VICTORY

41

Blessed is the one who perseveres under trial because, having stood the test, that person will receive the crown of life that the Lord has promised to those who love him.

JAMES 1:12 NIV

In the Bible, the person going through a great trial is the person next in line for a great victory.

Consider Gideon: Gideon and his family were among the Israelites who Moses led out of Egypt, but because the people did not obey the Lord, God allowed them to be taken captive by the Midianites for seven years. For seven years, the Israelites could not get ahead. Every time they planted crops or were able to purchase a sheep, goat, or ox, the Midianites would invade them and destroy everything. Gideon was going through this great trial, living an impoverished life, when God showed up and called him a "mighty man of valor" (Judges 6:12). Gideon's great trial was about to produce his great victory. God used Gideon to defeat the enemies of Israel—thousands and thousands of them—with a mere 300 men. When God is on your side, pity the other side!

Great victory is the three Hebrew men shouting at Nebuchadnezzar, the most powerful man on earth at the time: "... our God whom we serve is able to deliver us from the burning fiery furnace, and He will deliver us from your hand, O king" (Daniel 3:17). They didn't bend. They didn't bow. They did not burn. They walked out without the smell of smoke upon them, because the Holy One of Israel walked through that fire with them. When you get in real trouble, God doesn't send someone else, He shows up Himself!

You have probably heard the story of Daniel. Daniel was a governor, who the king was considering setting over the entire realm because God was with him. But many others did not want to see this happen. They devised a plan to trap Daniel so that the king would be forced to kill him. Everything went according to their plan. Daniel was caught worshipping God instead of King Darius, and Darius was forced to throw him into the lions' den. But Daniel's greatest trial was about to give God a great victory! King Darius was worried sick for Daniel's life, but Daniel was fast asleep with his head on the belly of a lion. In the morning, when King Darius called to Daniel, Daniel answered: "My God sent His angel and shut the lions' mouths, so that they have not hurt me, because I was found innocent before Him; and also, O king, I have done no wrong before you" (Daniel 6:22). A great victory indeed!

In Acts 16:23–40, Paul and Silas experienced a great victory as they sang in the Roman prison after being beaten, singing as a mighty earthquake set the prisoners free. Paul and Silas were set free and their jailer came out saying, "What must I do to be saved?" That is a great victory!

PRAYER

In Jesus' name, I come before You, Lord, asking for Your help. I declare that great victory will come from this great trial because You are with me, mighty God of Israel! Amen.

WHERE IS GOD IN THE STORM?

42

And behold, there arose a great storm on the sea, so that the boat was being swamped by the waves; but he was asleep.

MATTHEW 8:24 RSV

"... there arose a great storm on the sea." The Greek word for *storm* in this passage is *seismos*, which means there was an earthquake on the Sea of Galilee. The New King James Version says, "And suddenly a great tempest arose on the sea, so that the boat was covered with the waves." "Suddenly" tells us that the storm came instantly. The Jordan valley, with its two mountain ranges, forms a massive wind tunnel that empties into the Sea of Galilee. One minute the Sea of Galilee can be calm, and the next, because of that wind tunnel, you can see white caps.

Storms in life are much like storms on the Sea of Galilee. They come suddenly, instantly, like lightning out of the blue. You get a phone call from the hospital telling you that your child has just been involved in a serious automobile accident. Your X-ray shows a raging disease taking over your body. Your spouse walks in, and out of the blue says, "I want a divorce." Your boss walks in, and says, "The company is downsizing; your job is gone;" and there goes your dreams of retirement, of sending your kids to college, of paying off your mortgage. During all this, the devil puts in your brain, "Where is God when all this is going down?" I will tell you where He is. He is taking a nap in your boat, waiting for you to ask Him to help you get through the storm.

Now when He got into a boat, His disciples followed Him. And suddenly a great tempest arose on the sea, so that the boat was covered with the waves. But He was asleep. Then His disciples came to Him and awoke Him, saying, "Lord, save us! We are perishing!" (Matthew 8:23–25).

The disciples attacked Jesus with their version of pity-party Christianity. They went to Him and said, "Don't you see the mess we're in?! You sent us out here. We followed you. Now you're asleep in the boat! Some Rabbi you are! We are going to change synagogues as soon as we get to shore!" Sound familiar?

> *But He said to them, "Why are you fearful, O you of little faith?" Then He arose and rebuked the winds and the sea, and there was a great calm. So the men marveled, saying, "Who can this be, that even the winds and the sea obey Him?"* (Matthew 8:26–27).

Jesus said, "O you of little faith. You've seen Me heal the sick. You've seen Me turn water into wine. You saw Me open blind eyes. You saw Me make a lame man walk. You saw Me feed 5,000 men from a boy's sack lunch, and that was just yesterday! And now you're worried about a little water?! O ye of little faith. I AM the master of the storm. I AM the anchor of your soul. I AM the conqueror of the wind and the waves. I AM the mighty God, the Prince of Peace. And I AM in the boat with you!"

PRAYER

Jesus, Prince of Peace, I know that in every storm that comes suddenly upon my life I need not be afraid because You are there with me and You will help me reach the other side. I call upon You, today, the Great I AM! Amen.

DO-IT-NOW FAITH

43

Now faith is the substance of things hoped for, the evidence of things not seen.

HEBREWS 11:1

Do you read the Bible verses for each day? Be honest. I read a magazine article that said 92 percent of the American people lie on a regular basis. And those were just the ones who admitted it!

You are never going to get the full blessing of God if you skip over His Word. Half the work? Half the blessing! That's a fact.

I'm going to repeat today's verse because it is that important. You can go back and read it, but then come back here and read it again. Maybe you'll be lucky, and God will give you double for your trouble! Here it is: "Faith is the substance of things hoped for, the evidence of things not seen." I want to point out two words in that scripture: "substance" and "evidence." (You better go back and read it a third time just so you get it!)

My friend, faith is not a mystical something. Faith is not a rabbit's foot. But faith has substance, and it has evidence. The Bible has _evidence_ of all the miracles of God. You have _evidence_ in your life of how God has showed up for you in the past. This is the _evidence_. And when we have the faith that everything that God has done in the Bible and in our past He can do now—that is the _substance_.

Does the Bible say God helped the children of Israel? Has He helped you before? He can do it now.

Does the Bible say God provided for the children of Israel when they wandered in the desert? Has He provided for you before? He'll do it again.

Does the Bible say God healed the sick and brought health to their bodies? Has He healed you before? He can heal you now.

Does the Bible say God parted waters and made a way where there was no way? Has He opened closed doors for you before? He can open those doors now.

Does the Bible say God gave victory to the underdogs in the fight? Has He shaken the mountains of impossibility for you before? He can do it now.

Does the Bible say God carries the burdens of His children? Has He lifted your burdens before? He can do it now.

And, He'll do it again and again and again, because He never fails!

Do you need a miracle? Have faith in God. Not just faith that God exists, or that the Bible is true, but faith that the things God did in the past He will do for you now. Anybody can pray, "O God, do it sometime if it be Your will." It takes a person of faith to say, "Do it now."

PRAYER

Heavenly Father, I have do-it-now faith! I believe You can do it. You have done it in the past, and I believe You'll do it now! I receive my miracle, in Jesus' name! Amen.

REJECTION AND RESENTMENT

44

The spirit of a man will sustain him in sickness, but who can bear a broken spirit?

PROVERBS 18:14

As a teenager, I lived in a state of emotional war with my father, who was an ordained minister. I lived for sports. If it was round, I tried to hit it. If it was oblong, I tried to kick it. I was a four-sport letterman in middle school, and a starter all through high school and at university. Yet my father never came to a game, never asked me about a game, wasn't even curious why I made the newspaper. I resented him to the core. So, I know something about rejection.

Some of you feel rejected by a spouse who was unfaithful or who asked for a divorce. Some of you feel rejection and resentment because you were passed over for a promotion at work. Maybe you were left at the front door of an orphanage by your mother who never came back for you. Perhaps you were that pregnant mother, rejected by the child's father, and unknowingly passed on that spirit of rejection to your child.

I think judgment day is going to be filled with shocking revelations. You do not know the anguish, the heartache, the horror, that a person sitting next to you has lived through. You do not know the anguish of the heart of the people you pass on the street or in the hallway, the torment of their mind, the tears they have shed because of the desperation of their soul.

But know this: Jesus loved us before we loved Him, and He commands us to love one another as He has loved us (see John 15:12). Love is not what you say; love is what you do. I don't care how loud you sing or how big your spiritual accomplishments. If you do not demonstrate the love of God to others, you are a hypocrite of the highest order. Paul explains it this way in 1 Corinthians 13:

> *If I speak in the tongues of men or of angels, but do not have love, I am only a resounding gong or a clanging cymbal. If I have the gift of prophecy and can fathom all mysteries and all knowledge, and if I have a faith that can move mountains, but do not have love, I am nothing. If I give all I possess to the poor and give over my body to hardship that I may boast, but do not have love, I gain nothing* (1 Corinthians 13:1–3 NIV).

Don't be a nothing. Don't allow anyone who God puts on your path go another day without experiencing the love of God through you. Let us today walk in paths where there is no rejection but only God's eternal love and divine acceptance for all.

PRAYER

God, I refuse to let the rejection and resentment of my past prevent me from walking in love. Give me the strength and grace to show Your eternal love and divine acceptance to the people You put on my path today. In Jesus' name; Amen.

RECEIVE YOUR INHERITANCE

45

Instead of your shame you shall have double honor, and instead of confusion they shall rejoice in their portion. Therefore in their land they shall possess double; everlasting joy shall be theirs.

ISAIAH 61:7

Spectators walked by and mocked our Redeemer as He hung naked on a Roman cross with spittle dripping off His face and His precious blood dripping into the sands of Calvary. Mary, his mother, knelt before Him, sobbing. Her Son, who was pure and holy, was crucified with thieves. His trial was rigged. The Roman government conspired to kill Jesus Christ. In His closing statement to His Father, Jesus said, "My God, My God, why have You forsaken Me?" (Mark 15:34).

This is the only time in Scripture that Jesus called Him, "God." Every other time, it was "Father" or "My Father." But God was not looking at Jesus and Jesus knew it. Why? Because Jesus had taken our sin and God could not look upon it. When Jesus died, He took your sin, your suffering, your resentment, your rage. He took everything that torments you. He buried it all in the deepest sea, never to be remembered anymore. He bore your pain and your rejection. It is finished!

The prophet Isaiah saw the rejection of Jesus 700 years before it was ever accomplished by the Roman army on a hill outside Jerusalem. Isaiah 50:6 says, "I gave My back to those who struck Me, and My cheeks to those who plucked out the beard; I did not hide My face from shame and spitting." That is rejection. That is hatred.

What does God offer those in the 21st century who suffer from rejection and resentment? Isaiah writes,

Instead of your shame you will have a

double portion, and instead of humili-
ation they will shout for joy over their
portion. Therefore they will possess a
double portion in their land, everlasting
joy will be theirs (Isaiah 61:7 NASB).

What is your inheritance? Everlasting joy. He took our sickness and gave us healing. He took our poverty and gave us the blessings of Abraham. He took our sin and gave us forgiveness. He took our shame and humiliation and gave us joy. You can substitute all your rejection for the joy of the Lord.

We were outcast, but He adopted us. We were rejected, but He made us royal, kings and priests unto God, sons and daughters of Zion. We are ambassadors of Jesus Christ. He has turned our sorrow into joy. He has turned our mourning into dancing. He has turned our shame into highest honor. He has transformed our rejection into glory. He will set you free from the fear of tomorrow and the pain of the past. He will turn your darkest night into glorious day. Your sobs will become shouts of joy. Your failure will become the foundation of your success. Your prosperity is coming without limit. Give God praise!

PRAYER

God, I receive my inheritance from You this day—a double portion of exceeding joy, a spiritual recompense for all my troubles. I know that You are for me and no enemy can prosper against me! In Jesus' name; Amen.

SAINT PAUL'S PENICILLIN

46

For our light affliction, which is but for a moment, is working for us a far more exceeding and eternal weight of glory.

2 CORINTHIANS 4:17

Paul was beaten and left for dead. Christians turned their back on him. The Roman government put him in jail. He was in jail more than he was out of jail. The Corinthians mocked his teaching. He was bitten by snakes. He was shipwrecked. Yet, he calls those "light afflictions" and "momentary troubles." How could he stay so positive? Because he had a dose of what I like to call, "St. Paul's penicillin."

Saint Paul's penicillin for your troubles is this: "... forgetting those things which are behind and reaching forward to those things which are ahead" (Philippians 3:13). That is the key. Forget the past and focus on the higher calling. Don't even think about it. It's not worth thinking about in light of what heaven has for you. Some of you don't want to forget, but Paul said, "I press toward the goal for the prize of the upward call of God in Christ Jesus" (v. 14). You can't press upward if you insist on staying down in the dumps. You have to keep your eye on the prize, which is heaven-bound.

> *Therefore we also, since we are surrounded by so great a cloud of witnesses, let us lay aside every weight, and the sin which so easily ensnares us, and let us run with endurance the race that is set before us, looking unto Jesus, the author and finisher of our faith, who for the joy that was set before Him endured the cross, despising the shame, and has sat down at the right hand of the throne of God* (Hebrews 12:1–2).

Run the race with endurance. Run it with patience. Be an overcomer. Wipe the tears out of your eyes because the prize is greater than the burden. Jesus knew that. Jesus taught that. Jesus endured the Cross with joy because He knew "an eternal weight of glory far beyond all comparison" (2 Corinthians 4:17 NASB) was waiting for Him.

Life is a way; it is a road, not a parking lot. Life is a school; it is not a cemetery. Life is an arena; it's not a bleacher seat where you watch life go by. Life is for growth, for movement, for action, for progress. Stop living life looking through a rear view mirror. Take a dose of St. Paul's penicillin. Get up and get moving, forgetting those things which are behind. Rejoice ever more and give thanks in everything because you know the heavenly prize that is yours in Christ Jesus.

PRAYER

Jesus, I am taking a page out of Your book today. I am pressing through my storms, because I know that in the long run I will see that they are light and momentary troubles and nothing compared to the glory that is mine in You. Amen.

WHAT IS MAKING YOU SICK?

47

For as he thinks in his heart, so is he ...

PROVERBS 23:7

Medical science has proven that resentment can physically and mentally destroy you. Our mind and body are so connected that they affect the well-being of each other. Doctors call it "psychosomatic." *Psycho*, referring to your brain, and *somatic* to your body. In other words, if you think it, you'll become it.

If your body gets sick, you can make your mind sick just by thinking about being sick. The reverse is also true. If your mind is sick, dwelling on rejection, failure, bitterness, or betrayal, you can make your body sick. But if you focus on God being with you and tell yourself you are getting better, if you focus on God's plans for you—plans for "a future and a hope" (Jeremiah 29:11)—then your mind can actually heal your body. Your positive thoughts can keep you from getting sick.

A doctor once looked me in the eye and said, "One in a million, those are the odds that you will get over what you've got." And I said, "I'm going to be that one in a million!" God put that in my heart. I began to say it, and my heart began to believe it, and my body began to respond to it. Speak it, believe it, and God will bring it to pass. Through the faith you have, God will do it.

Solomon, the wisest man who ever lived, said, "A merry heart does good, like medicine ..." (Proverbs 17:22). If you want to be happy, then continually surrender life's heartaches, trials, and disappointments, continually place all these things into the hands of God. The

Bible says, "casting all your care upon Him, for He cares for you" (1 Peter 5:7). All your care. Every care. That doesn't mean you keep some of them. You let them ALL go, every care, because He wants to carry it, and He will if you'll turn loose of it.

Are your fists wrapped around your troubles? Let them loose. Don't make God use a crowbar to pry them out of your hands. God will never force you to open your hand. He wants you to give it freely to Him. God will never force you to let go of your resentments and rejection. You must choose to let them go. Do it today before your mind is corrupted and your body becomes sick. Turn it loose. Don't let resentment and bitterness make you sick!

PRAYER

Lord, I declare that You are my Jehovah Rapha, the Lord Who Heals me. I believe what Your Word says in Proverbs 16:24 that, "Pleasant words are like a honeycomb, sweetness to the soul and health to the bones." My mind and body are connected, and I will keep them both in good health, as is pleasing to You, O Lord, my Rock and my Redeemer! In Jesus' name; Amen.

HISTORY REPEATING

48

*If an enemy
were insulting
me, I could
endure it; if a
foe were rising
against me, I
could hide. But
it is you, a man
like myself, my
companion, my
close friend.*

PSALM 55:12–13 NIV

Look at the bloody road of betrayal in history. On the Ides of March, Julius Caesar was stabbed 23 times by those he called friends. Historical lore, as portrayed by Shakespeare, says that Caesar's last words before bleeding to death were, "You too, Brutus?"

Jesus of Nazareth gathered his 12 disciples into the Upper Room for the Last Supper. He looked at them and said, "Did I not choose you, the 12, and one of you is a devil?" (John 6:70). Judas, the betrayer, slipped out into the darkness to sell the Son of God for thirty pieces of silver, the price of a slave.

Saint Paul, who wrote most of the New Testament, was beaten by the Roman cat-of-nine-tails until the blood ran in streams down his back. Yet Saint Paul's deepest scars were not given to him by the Romans. They were the rejection and betrayal of the fellow believers to whom he ministered: "for Demas has forsaken me, having loved this present world, and has departed for Thessalonica—Crescens for Galatia, Titus for Dalmatia" (2 Timothy 4:10). Demas, Crescens, and Titus had all abandoned him. Luke alone remained (v. 11).

Christians betray one another. Every act of gossip and tale bearing on your part is betrayal. If you are not an eyewitness, you are a false witness. Remember, those who talk to you about others will talk to others about you. Sooner or later, you're going to have a dear friend reject, betray, or gossip about you. It will be someone close to you, who you would never dream would do that to you. It will happen, and if you let it fester in your soul it will destroy your mind. It will crucify your hope. It will make your life bitter.

The best thing you can do is erase it then replace it with the joy of the Lord that "maketh rich and addeth no sorrow" (Proverbs 10:22 KJV). Turn it loose. Let it go. Get it out of your life, out of your speech, and out of your mind. Forget it and move on. It won't be easy. You won't want to let them get away with it. You'll want to harbor bitter resentment. But trust God to bring about your deliverance, your peace, your strength in adversity. Even when others betray you, He will stick closer to you than a brother.

PRAYER

God, I am ready for a new beginning, where rejection and the pain that it has caused and the resentment that it has tolerated is no longer in my speech, spirit, or mind. Forgive me for the times that I have betrayed You and others through gossip and unkind words. Help me forget the times that those I call friends have betrayed me. By Your grace, I can have a new beginning! I will walk in the love and the joy and the peace that You have made possible for me to have, even in the storm. In Jesus' name; Amen.

49

So when Jesus had received the sour wine, He said, "It is finished!" And bowing His head, He gave up His spirit.

JOHN 19:30

Many of you have created a prison. Brick by brick, hurt by hurt, tear by tear, scar by scar, the walls of the prison have been built by abuse, real or imaginary. Those walls scream of rejection and resentment. Those walls will become filled with rage. You want to escape but you don't know how.

The Bible has the answer. It says:

> ... *looking unto Jesus, the author and finisher of our faith, who for the joy that was set before Him endured the cross, despising the shame, and has sat down at the right hand of the throne of God* (Hebrews 12:2).

Look at Jesus. Fix your eyes on Him. Jesus took your shame to the Cross and put an end to it. Jesus, the Son of God, the King of the universe, God With Us, the hope of glory, has experienced your pain. You might think no one knows how you feel, but Jesus does. He knows and He understands. In fact, Jesus knew how you would feel before you were ever born, and He despised the shame that you would experience so much that He bore your suffering. He bore your resentment and your rage. And when He said, "It is finished," it was over forever. It was over by the power of the blood of the Cross. He is the "author *and* finisher of our faith," the first *and* the last, the beginning *and* the end.

Jesus said in Matthew 11:

> *"Come to Me, all you who labor and are heavy laden, and I will give you rest. Take My yoke upon you and learn from*

Me, for I am gentle and lowly in heart, and you will find rest for your souls. For My yoke is easy and My burden is light" (vv. 28–30).

If your burdens are heavy, come to Jesus. If you are tired to the point of exhaustion, come to Jesus. If you are still carrying around shame, guilt, resentment, rage at feeling rejected—come to Jesus. In Him is peace, rest, and release from all those burdens that are weighing you down. He has paid the price for all of it so that you can live "freely and lightly" in the "unforced rhythms of grace" (Matthew 11:28–30 MSG). You don't have to suffer any more. With a word, He will take it off your shoulders. Release it. Let it go; holding on is not doing you any good. Give it to Him!

PRAYER

Jesus, my Savior, You conquered death, hell, and the grave. I give You my burdens; I give You my shame. You have taken them to the Cross and declared "It is finished." Shame has no hold on me! It is finished. I am free! Amen.

WHY ARE YOU FEARFUL?

50

But He said to them, "Why are you fearful, O you of little faith?" Then He arose and rebuked the winds and the sea, and there was a great calm.

MATTHEW 8:26

In Matthew, the 12 disciples are on the Sea of Galilee. God Almighty, in the form of Jesus Christ, is in the boat with them when a storm comes up. The storm was no surprise to Jesus. He had led the disciples into the storm. He had gotten into the boat with them. And He had one goal in mind: to increase their faith.

> *Now when He got into a boat, His disciples followed Him. And suddenly a great tempest arose on the sea, so that the boat was covered with the waves. But He was asleep. Then His disciples came to Him and awoke Him, saying, "Lord, save us! We are perishing!" But He said to them, "Why are you fearful, O you of little faith?" Then He arose and rebuked the winds and the sea, and there was a great calm. So the men marveled, saying, "Who can this be, that even the winds and the sea obey Him?"* (Matthew 8:23–27).

Every storm is God's seminar on faith for you. His question to the disciples is the same question that God is asking most of you right now: "Why are you fearful?" That is a compelling question. The Creator of heaven and earth was in the boat with them, yet they were afraid. The disciples were screaming in fear, and Jesus was asleep.

Think about that. The storm did not catch Jesus by surprise. He knew it would come, and yet He went to sleep. Why? Because He sent the disciples into the storm to develop them, to teach them that even though they had been raised on this sea, they still needed Him in every facet of their lives. If you will not talk to God in times of peace and tranquility, God will send you a storm to remind you that you need Him, and so He can hear your voice screaming, "Help!"

This message from the Word of God is relevant to every person. How do I know? Answer this one simple question: How many of you have ever been in trouble? I guarantee I have 100 percent participation! If you're not in a storm of trouble right now, chances are good you either just came out of one or you are headed in that direction.

Why does God allow storms in our lives? To teach us that we need Him every day and every hour of our lives. Storms demonstrate His power, His might, His majesty, His absolute control over all the universe. God uses storms to shake us out of our comfort zones into a position of complete dependence upon Him. God will take you to a place where, if He doesn't come through, you won't make it. That's when you discover how good God is!

PRAYER

Holy Spirit, help me to see that storms are meant to increase my faith, not drown me in my own fears. No matter what storm I am going through, I know that You are in the boat with me; I need not be afraid. In Jesus' name; Amen.

FACE YOUR FEARS

51

I sought the LORD, and He heard me, and delivered me from all my fears.

PSALM 34:4

Did you know that America's greatest fear is the fear of public speaking? Luckily, I conquered this fear early on. I have my mother and her persistent guidance to thank for that. When I was six years old, my mother told me I was going to sing a solo the next day during the main worship service. It was a song I'd never heard, but she insisted that I learn it and sing it perfectly the next day. The next morning, when it was my turn to sing, I got up on stage and stood behind the pulpit. Now, I could barely see my father over the pulpit it was so large, so there was no way anyone could see even a hair on my six-year-old head. I couldn't see the congregation and they couldn't see me. That was my plan! However, my persistent mother walked up on the platform, pulled me out from behind the pulpit and stood me front and center. Then she whispered to me, "Stare at the clock if you are nervous." It was 11:15 a.m. I'll never forget the time because I sang all three verses to the clock! When the song was over, and I sat back down in the pews, I realized: I was still alive! I had faced a new fear and I was changed forever.

That story teaches us, in order to conquer fear, we must first admit our fears and then face them head on. Fear is a fact of life. The most common and most subtle of all human diseases is fear. Public speaking might be on your list of fears, but there are countless others that might threaten to immobilize you: fear of the future, fear of danger, fear of the past. Some fear the loss of a job, the loss of their health, criticism from others, exposure, failure. There is the fear of being disliked, the fear of death, fear of the unknown.

This era of human history is the era of anxiety and fear. But we need not look further than the Bible to encourage us in times of fear. Listen to the voice of God through King David: "Yea, though I walk through the valley of the shadow of death, I will fear no evil; for You are with me; Your rod and Your staff, they comfort me" (Psalm 23:4). Isaiah wrote, "Behold, God is my salvation, I will trust and not be afraid; 'For Yah, the LORD, is my strength and song; He also has become my salvation'" (Isaiah 12:2). The New Testament begins with an angel telling the Virgin Mary, "Do not be afraid, Mary, for you have found favor with God" (Luke 1:30). In Mary's time, when a girl was found to be pregnant without a husband she was stoned to death. Mary had every reason to be fearful. But the angel told her to "fear not."

Fear is a fact, but it doesn't have to rule your life. Acknowledge your fears and face them head on in the strength and courage of God who "has not given us a spirit of fear, but of power and of love and of a sound mind" (2 Timothy 1:7).

PRAYER

Lord, I declare that I will not be afraid. I can face my fears head on, because You are with me. You are the Alpha and the Omega, the Beginning and the End, who is and who was and who is to come, the Almighty! In Jesus' name; Amen.

TWO KINDS OF FEAR

52

For God has not given us a spirit of fear, but of power and of love and of a sound mind.

2 TIMOTHY 1:7

There are two kinds of fear. There is the emotion of fear, which is God-given. Then there's the spirit of fear, which comes from the prince of darkness. God has not given us the spirit of fear.

Let me give you an example of the emotion of fear, the healthy fear that God gives to every human being. When I was eight years old, my father killed a panther behind our house. Two nights later my parents left the house to go visit church members. Before they left the house, my mother asked me to burn the trash while they were gone. In those days, when you lived in the country, you didn't have trash pick-up. You had a designated burn pile about 50 yards behind the house. So, I took the trash out, like mother asked, but just before I was about to light it, I heard a hiss. I don't even remember my feet hitting the ground I took off so fast for the house. I thought for sure I was lunch meat for that panther's relatives. I got to the back of the house and the door was locked. Locked! I hit the window pane and broke it, reaching in to unlock the door. It didn't dawn on me until I was safely inside, with the door shut behind me, that if it had been a real panther, I never would have been able to outrun it. Which is when I heard my older brother laughing.

That is an example of the emotion of fear. The good fear that God gives us to preserve our lives, to help us reach our objectives. Another example might be paying taxes. Why do you pay taxes? Because you love to send checks to the IRS? I don't think so. It's because you fear being thrown in prison. Why do you take out fire insurance? Because you love your insurance agent? I don't think so. It's because you fear a fire could wipe you out. Why do you lock the doors of your house? Because you fear murderers, thieves, and rapists will come in and you want to protect yourself. God gives you the emotion of fear to help you.

But there is another type of fear, and that is the spirit of fear, which comes from the prince of darkness. Psychiatrists describe these abnormal, irrational, mind-crippling fears as "phobias." Psychologists say there are 75 different kinds of phobias, fears that are so compelling and encompassing that they destroy your peace of mind, your health, your relationships, and any possibility of having a normal, happy life. God tells us to rebuke those fears, because they have no place in our lives. Those fears are not from God. If the spirit of fear is threatening to take over your life, fight back with the Spirit of Christ that says, "Get behind Me, Satan! You are an offense to Me, for you are not mindful of the things of God ..." (Matthew 16:23).

PRAYER

Father God, I believe that You have not given me a spirit of fear, but of power and of love and of a sound mind. Fear cannot control me. Help me enjoy my life, Lord, without the dread of fear. In Jesus' name; Amen.

"ADAM, WHERE ARE YOU?"

53

Then the LORD God called to Adam and said to him, "Where are you?"

GENESIS 3:9

The spirit of fear was born in the Garden of Eden as a product of sin. Adam was not afraid of God until he sinned. He walked and talked with God, just like a child would talk to his father. But when Adam sinned, he heard the voice of God say, "Adam, where are you?"

Is God saying that to you today? Is He calling your name and asking, "Where are you? Where are you spiritually? Why have you walked away from Me? Why do you think you can hide from Me?"

Let me tell you something: when God asks that question, He's not looking for information; He knows where you are. He knows how you are. He knows what you're doing and what you've done. What He is really asking is for you to get yourself squared away to face Him on the day that you give an account for your life.

Adam responded to God's question with: "I heard Your voice in the garden, and I was afraid because I was naked; and I hid myself" (Genesis 3:10). Sin gives fear a license to rule your life. Adam sinned, and became afraid. And that fear made him keep sinning, making excuses for his sin, as he grew more and more afraid. Learn from Adam what not to do when sin and fear enter your life. Whenever the spirit of fear begins to attack your mind or comes into your speech, recognize it and cast it out. Stop it! Don't think it. Don't speak it. Don't act upon it. Act upon the faith that God has given you. Repent, rebuke, rejoice!

King David wrote in Psalm 119:11, "Your word

I have hidden in my heart, that I might not sin against You." You can stop sin in its tracks by filling ourselves up on the Word of God. Don't hide from God; hide His Word in your heart. Don't give way to sin which gives way to fear. Don't let it linger; stop it in its tracks. Repent of your sin. Rebuke the devil that tries to take you down with the spirit of fear. And rejoice in God, your Savior. Study God's promises so that when God comes looking for you, you can say, like Isaiah did, "Here am I! Send me" (Isaiah 6:8).

PRAYER

Heavenly Father, help me recognize the spirit of fear in my life. Give me the courage to crush it with Your Word. I declare that I am who the Bible says I am. I can have what the Bible says I can have. I can do what the Bible says I can do. I have the power and might to achieve, climb the highest mountain, and defeat the largest enemy, because greater is He who is in me than he who is in the world. Yes, and Amen!

FEAR AND SIN

54

The fear of the LORD is the beginning of knowledge, but fools despise wisdom and instruction.

PROVERBS 1:7

God planted the emotion of fear in our mortal nature to make us uneasy with sin. Sin needs to be called sin. It will not just go away. It must be repented of and forsaken.

Why has human trafficking become such an issue in our day? Because there is no fear of God. Why are people being shot in the streets? Because there is no fear of God. Why is this nation saturated with drive-by shootings, corruption, anarchy? Because there is no fear of God. Why are thousands of babies being aborted every day in America? Because there is no fear of God. We've kicked the Prince of Peace out of our schools and now they have become a war zone of death and suffering. Why fear God? Because some day you're going to have to stand in God's presence and give an account for your life. If thieves, murderers, rapists, and human traffickers truly believed they were going to face God in the Judgment Seat, then these crimes would cease to exist.

Matthew's Gospel says,

> *"Not everyone who says to Me, 'Lord, Lord,' shall enter the kingdom of heaven, but he who does the will of My Father in heaven. Many will say to Me in that day, 'Lord, Lord, have we not prophesied in Your name, cast out demons in Your name, and done many wonders in Your name?' And then I will declare to them, 'I never knew you; depart from Me, you who practice lawlessness!'"* (Matthew 7:21–23).

The leaders of the church were the ones performing miracles at that time, so Jesus was clearly speaking to regular church attenders in this passage. Yet, Jesus said, "I never knew you. You did things with My power and in My name, but you personally never submitted to Me."

God requires our submission, repentance, and fear of Him. King David says in Psalm 119, "My flesh trembles for fear of You, and I am afraid of Your judgments" (Psalm 119:120). His son Solomon says in Proverbs 1:7, "The fear of the Lord is the beginning of knowledge ..." David obviously taught his son the importance of respecting God. Solomon was the wisest man who ever lived for one key reason: he feared the Lord.

> Now therefore, be wise, O kings; be instructed, you judges of the earth. Serve the LORD with fear, and rejoice with trembling. Kiss the Son, lest He be angry, and you perish in the way, when His wrath is kindled but a little. Blessed are all those who put their trust in Him (Psalm 2:10–12).

PRAYER

Lord, I come to You with a repentant heart. I know that one day I will be standing before You, giving an account of all my sins. I tremble for fear of Your judgment, knowing that I am deserving of death. I rejoice with trembling and give thanks for Your mercy and kindness, O God, and receive the gift of Your Son Jesus', my Savior. In Jesus' name; Amen.

BURN THE BOATS

55

Then Caleb quieted the people before Moses, and said, "Let us go up at once and take possession, for we are well able to overcome it."

NUMBERS 13:30

One of my favorite stories in history begins in 1519 when an extraordinary man set sail on the final leg of a voyage from the shores of Cuba to the Yucatan Peninsula. His name was Hernán Cortés, and his mission was to capture the world's richest treasure, a treasure of gold, silver, jewels, and artifacts that were truly wealth unmeasured. This treasure had been held by the same army for 600 years. Army after army, conqueror after conqueror, had tried to take it and failed.

Cortés had 11 ships, 500 soldiers, 100 sailors, and 16 horses. He got his army together and set out to retrieve the treasure, but halfway through the voyage many of the soldiers and sailors became fearful. They knew that countless others had tried and failed. Cortés listened patiently to their laments, and when they finally arrived at the Yucatan Peninsula, he gathered all his frightened men on the shore. They grew quiet, waiting for Cortés to confirm that their fears were justified and to assure them that they would turn around and head home peacefully. Instead Cortés said: "Burn the boats."

What?!

"Burn the boats."

They must have thought him mad; but Cortés was their commanding officer, so they obeyed his command and burned every boat that they had sailed in on. When they were finished, Cortés said, "If we go home, we're going home in *their* boats." This was all the motivation the men needed. Cortés's men fought furiously.

They knew their only choice was to take the treasure and win the fight. And for the first time in 600 years, the treasure was taken. Why? Because burning the boats stirred up a confidence and a healthy fear in them.

I believe this is how the story could have turned out for the Israelites when they left Egypt. I don't think they had to wander in the wilderness for 40 years before entering the Promised Land. When Moses sent 12 men to spy out the land, Joshua and Caleb returned with the report that they were well able to overcome the giants that guard the land of milk and honey! But the other ten men reported: "we were like grasshoppers in our own sight, and so we were in their sight" (Numbers 13:33). Fear is contagious. The children of Israel refused to listen to Joshua and Caleb and found themselves living off manna instead of the fruit of the Promised Land.

When fear grabs you by the throat, send faith to answer: "Burn the boats!" Burn your fears. Burn your excuses. Burn your insecurities. Burn your lack of confidence. Get away from your negative friends. Break out of your negative environment. Burn it all and choose to trust the Creator of the Universe.

PRAYER

God, I refuse to give in to fear. I refuse to let fear steal from my life the promises You have for me. I am confident in Christ. You are with me in my day of battle. I will burn the boats of fear and insecurity in my life and put my trust in You! In Jesus' name; Amen.

FAITH OVER FEAR

56

That is true. They were broken off because of their unbelief, but you stand fast only through faith. So do not become proud, but fear.

ROMANS 11:20 ESV

Let me tell you a little secret that I have learned in life: your greatest crisis will come from the *fear of trouble*, not the presence of trouble. Did you hear that? Your greatest crisis will come from the FEAR of trouble, NOT the presence of trouble. Your greatest trials and storms, your hardest days will all take place in your mind, not in reality. Which means that you can overcome life's greatest battles with faith. Faith over fear!

Fear says you're too tired to try again, too weak to win, too exhausted to endure. But faith shouts back: "I am more than a conqueror through Christ! (See Romans 8:37.) Nothing is impossible with God on my side!" (See Luke 1:37.) And, "those who wait on the LORD shall renew their strength; they shall mount up with wings like eagles, they shall run and not be weary, they shall walk and not faint" (Isaiah 40:31).

Fear says the disease in your body is fatal. The truth is, disease has killed its thousands, but the spirit of fear has killed its tens of thousands. You must fight back with faith immediately, before the spirit of fear takes hold! Faith shouts back: "I shall live and not die!" (See Psalm 118:17.) "By His stripes, I am healed!" (See Isaiah 53:5.) "Jesus Christ is still the Great Physician, and right now, His healing powers are at work in my life!"

Fear says your business is going to fail. Faith shouts back: "The Lord makes me increase and abound!" (See 1 Thessalonians 3:12.)

Fear will break your spirit. It will destroy your defenses. It will disarm you in the day of battle.

It will bring terror to you on your death bed. Regardless of your profession of faith, if you live with the spirit of fear you are a practical atheist. You don't really believe what God says. But when you do believe what God says, the spirit of fear can no longer be a part of your life or your speech. It is GONE! Out of here! Replaced and overcome by faith, the strength of which it never stood a chance against. Even a mustard seed of faith is enough to conquer the spirit of fear: "Truly I tell you, if you have faith as small as a mustard seed, you can say to this mountain, 'Move from here to there,' and it will move. Nothing will be impossible for you" (Matthew 17:20 NIV).

PRAYER

Lord, I declare that every time fear tries to speak into my life, I will shout it down like the walls of Jericho. Fear doesn't stand a chance! I stand in awe of Your great and mighty works. You can do all things through even the tiniest grain of faith, and I can do all things through Christ who strengthens me. In Jesus' name; Amen and Amen!

57

For as by one man's disobedience many were made sinners, so also by one Man's obedience many will be made righteous. Moreover the law entered that the offense might abound. But where sin abounded, grace abounded much more, so that as sin reigned in death, even so grace might reign through righteousness to eternal life through Jesus Christ our Lord.

ROMANS 5:19–21

Every person has a dark page in their life. You are not the Lone Ranger. Everyone has a past. And everyone has that little voice that whispers in their ear, "God will never forgive you for that." But that voice is a liar! The Bible, through the pen of the Apostle Paul, says, "where sin abounded, grace abounded much more." God's grace is greater than all your sin. The proof is on the Cross.

When Jesus hung on the Cross, with the weight of all our sins upon Him, He said, "Father, forgive them, for they do not know what they do" (Luke 23:34). His grace is great enough to forgive the sins of those who crucified Him. If His grace is that great, surely you can believe that it is great enough to forgive your sins. Jesus was crucified between two thieves, men who deserved the punishment being inflicted upon them. Moments before taking his last breath, one of the men asked Jesus to "remember him" to His Father in heaven. The man's repentance was sincere, and so was Jesus' forgiveness. Jesus said to him, "Assuredly, I say to you, today you will be with Me in Paradise" (Luke 23:43). Where sin abounds, grace abounds much more. Great grace!

Don't let the devil torment you about your past. Your sins are buried in the deepest sea, never to be remembered: "He will again have compassion on us, and will subdue our iniquities. You will cast all our sins into the depths of the sea" (Micah 7:19). They are washed whiter than snow: "... Though your sins are like scarlet, they shall be as white as snow; though they are red like crimson, they shall be as wool" (Isaiah 1:18). Whatever you've done, God's grace is greater. I don't know what you've done, but it doesn't matter, because I know God's grace is greater. Your sins are gone; God's grace is greater!

PRAYER

Heavenly Father, in the name of the Lord Jesus Christ, I come before You today and give my fear to You. Those things that have tormented and haunted me, that thing in my past, I am no longer going to consider. I am no longer going to think fearfully. I am no longer going to speak fearfully. I am going to act with the boldness of a lion and accomplish the destiny You have for me. I believe You are for me therefore no one can be against me. And from this day forward, it is victory! Victory! Victory! by the authority of the resurrected Savior. Victory in Jesus' name; Amen!

FAITH IS THE VICTORY

58

For whatever is born of God overcomes the world. And this is the victory that has overcome the world—our faith. Who is he who overcomes the world, but he who believes that Jesus is the Son of God?

1 JOHN 5:4—5

Faith is the victory that overcomes the world. Our faith in Jesus Christ, the Son of God, is what overcomes the world. Hebrews 11:1 says, "Now faith is the substance of things hoped for, the evidence of things not seen." Faith starts out before you know how it's going to turn out. It is believing for victory, even when all the odds are stacked against you.

Faith drove Abraham to look for a city whose builder and maker was God; and he found it. Faith drove Moses into Pharaoh's court shouting, "Let my people go." It drove him through the Red Sea, through 40 years of sand and suffering to a land flowing with milk and honey. Faith drove Joshua through Jericho to claim the Promised Land. Faith drove David to face Goliath with these words: "You come to me with a sword, with a spear, and with a javelin. But I come to you in the name of the LORD of hosts, the God of the armies of Israel ..." (1 Samuel 17:45). Faith drove Paul and Silas to sing a song of victory in the midnight hour after being beaten by the Roman cat-of-nine tails and thrown into prison. Faith led Habakkuk to say, "The just shall live by faith" (2:4). Faith drove Martin Luther to nail his *95 Theses* to the door of the Roman Church, birthing the Protestant Reformation. When America was attacked by Japan on December 7, 1941, Americans gathered around the radio where they heard President Roosevelt say in faith, "We have nothing to fear but fear itself."

Faith can turn your desert into springs of living water. Faith can calm the troubled seas.

Faith can move mountains of impossibility. Faith is the victory that overcomes the world. Faith is the thing that gives you the strength to do the impossible. Faith is the thing that opens doors that can't be moved any other way. Faith says, "I can, because God says I can." Faith does not retreat when the fire starts; it walks through the fire without being burned. Faith is the evidence of things that aren't seen on earth, but God is birthing in heaven. Have faith and you have victory!

PRAYER

I believe in You, the Father Almighty, Creator of heaven and earth. I believe in Jesus Christ, Your only Son, and my Lord, who was conceived by the Holy Spirit and born of the Virgin Mary. He suffered under Pontius Pilate, was crucified, died, and was buried; He descended to hell. The third day He rose again from the dead. He ascended to heaven and is seated at the right hand of God the Father Almighty. From there He will come to judge the living and the dead. I believe in the Holy Spirit, the Holy Church, the communion of saints, the forgiveness of sins, the resurrection of the body, and the life everlasting. In Jesus' name; Amen.

SELF-FULFILLING PROPHECY

59

The fear of man brings a snare, but whoever trusts in the LORD shall be safe.

PROVERBS 29:25

I once heard a true story about a man named Nick. Nick was a strong, healthy railroad man. He got along with his fellow coworkers and was a reliable employee. But he had a deep-rooted fear that he would be locked inside a refrigerator boxcar.

One summer day, the railyard crew was told they could go home early. Everyone left, but Nick was accidentally locked in a refrigerator boxcar that was in the yard for repairs. His worst fear had come true! Nick panicked. He shouted and banged against the walls until his fists were bloody. He thought, if I don't get out of here, I will freeze to death! Shivering, he scratched a message to his wife: "I'm so cold. I'm getting numb. If I could just go to sleep. These may be my last words to you."

The next morning, the crew slid open the boxcar's door and found Nick's body. An autopsy revealed that he had every physical sign that he had frozen to death. But the boxcar had been in the yard for repairs because the car's refrigeration system was broken. The temperature inside the car had never gotten below 61 degrees.

That is how powerful fear can be. Fear can paralyze you. Fear can kill you. Fear can become a self-fulfilling prophecy. Paul writes to the Corinthian church: "No temptation has overtaken you except such as is common to man; but God is faithful, who will not allow you to be tempted beyond what you are able, but with the temptation will also make the way of escape, that you may be able to bear it" (1 Corinthians

10:13). You may be tempted to give your life over to fear but know that God will not place a greater burden on you than you are able to bear, and with every burden He always provides a way out.

What fears are you allowing to control your life, destroy your peace, steal the joy of the Lord that "maketh rich and addeth no sorrow"? What fear have you allowed into the theater of your mind to destroy the hope that you have for your future? What fear is ravaging your marriage? What fear is destroying your potential?

I want you to understand that the prince of darkness is in the misery business. The moment you allow fear to walk into your heart, mouth, mind, home, or office, you have opened the door to the prince of darkness who wants to destroy you. Proverbs 29:25 says, "The fear of man brings a snare ..." A snare is a trap, and that is exactly what the devil wants you to fall into. But you can overcome the prince of darkness when you receive the second half of that verse: "... but whoever trusts in the LORD shall be safe."

PRAYER

God, I believe that You are mighty to save. No matter what fears tempt to overtake me, You have given me a way out. That way out is simple trust in You to keep me safe! Lord, I believe. In Jesus' name; Amen.

60

God is not human, that he should lie, not a human being, that he should change his mind. Does he speak and then not act? Does he promise and not fulfill?

NUMBERS 23:19 NIV

When my daughter Sandy was eight years old, she wanted a dog more than anything. And not just any dog. She wanted a dog that could stay in the house. I put my foot down. Absolutely not! Dogs belong outside. At least that's the way I was raised. No dog was going to sleep in my house!

Well, one Sunday morning I preached a sermon about God granting the desires of your heart (see Psalm 20:4; Psalm 37:4). On the way home, Sandy said, "Dad, do you believe that what you preached this morning is the truth?" I said, "Absolutely, I believe it." She proceeded to tell me that the desire of her heart was to have a dog, a dog that lived in the house, and that God was going to give it to her. I asked her what kind of dog and she said, "A male Pomeranian." Pretty specific! But I knew this was the dog she wanted because the day before we had been in a pet shop where they were selling male Pomeranian dogs for $600. Well, there was no way I was paying $600 for a dog and she knew it! So, she said, "If someone gives me a male Pomeranian dog, will you let me keep it?" I quickly calculated in my head the chances that someone would give my eight-year-old daughter a $600 dog and figured the odds were in my favor. So, I said yes, if someone gave her the dog, she could keep it.

The next morning my wife called me at the church office and said, "Are you sitting down?" (You know that is code for "get ready to have your socks knocked off!") She proceeded to tell me that a neighbor had just called and offered to give Sandy a male Pomeranian puppy. I was livid! I felt set up! There was no way that less than 24 hours before we were talking about a male Pomeranian dog and now, completely unsolicited and out of the blue, a neighbor calls and asks if she can give that exact dog to my daughter. No way! Well, my wife told me I was welcome to call the neighbor and refuse the dog and then tell Sandy she couldn't keep it because I didn't believe what I had preached about God granting the desires of the heart. Obviously, we got the dog.

The Word of God contains 3,000 promises from God (the Father) to us (His children). He has given us the keys to the Kingdom: "And whatever things you ask in prayer, believing, you will receive" (Matthew 21:22). It isn't presumptuous to claim the promises of God; it's our right as His children!

PRAYER

God, You promise in Your Word that no good thing will You withhold from those who walk uprightly, and that You are a rewarder of those who diligently seek You. I boldly claim these promises for my life! In Jesus' name; Amen.

ABSOLUTE TRUTH

61

But the fearful, and unbelieving, and the abominable, and murderers, and whoremongers, and sorcerers, and idolaters, and all liars, shall have their part in the lake which burneth with fire and brimstone: which is the second death.

REVELATION 21:8 KJV

Did you know that fear is a sin? The book of Revelation says that "the fearful, and unbelieving" will be cast into hell. Think about that. Fear and unbelief are treason against God. If God is not truth, if He is not to be believed, then He is not fit to be God. But if you do worship Him as God, then you owe Him absolute allegiance. You must believe that what He says in the Bible is absolute truth. You will believe it to the point of death, because hell cannot stop you.

> *Do not fear any of those things which you are about to suffer. Indeed, the devil is about to throw some of you into prison, that you may be tested, and you will have tribulation ten days. Be faithful until death, and I will give you the crown of life* (Revelation 2:10).

God wants you to believe in Him and believe in His promises until your last breath. Believe Him when He says: "I will never leave you nor forsake you" (Deuteronomy 31:6). The Father is with you. The Son is with you. The Holy Spirit is in you. Greater is He that is in you than he that is in the world (see 1 John 4:4).

On the spiritual level, not to believe that God will keep His promises is practical atheism. You quote the Bible, but the moment a storm comes along, you are terrified. Why? Because you don't really believe that God will come to your aid. But faith is not believing that God can. Faith is believing that God *will*, and He will do it for you, and He will do it right now. That's faith!

Each of us always has two angels with us. The Bible says, "For He shall give His angels charge over you, to keep you in all your ways" (Psalm 91:11). The angels are with you. His anointing is with you. You are never alone. You are never without God. He knows your thoughts before you think them and your prayers before you ask them. Fear not, for He is with you. He is ready and willing to turn the forces of heaven loose to reshape the earth if necessary. You're His child. He will not abandon you. He will not let you go through the fire unless He goes with you. If the storm is greater than you are, it is not greater than God! He is with you. In the raging storm, He is with you. Be brave. Be bold. For the Lord your God is with you. Believe it as absolute truth.

PRAYER

Lord, I believe in the inerrancy of Your Word. You are not a man that You should lie. You are absolute Truth. If You say You will, You will. If You did it then You can do it today. You are the same yesterday, today, and forever. Thou art with me, I will not fear! In Jesus' name; Amen.

A WORTHLESS BUSH

62

And the Angel of the LORD appeared to him in a flame of fire from the midst of a bush. So he looked, and behold, the bush was burning with fire, but the bush was not consumed.

EXODUS 3:2

God's strength is manifested in crisis. When God shows up and manifests His power in you, you can do things that you would never believe you could do. It is not your power, but God's at work within you, allowing you to do the impossible.

God's strength was poured into Samson as he ripped the jaws of a lion like tissue paper.

> *So Samson went down to Timnah with his father and mother, and came to the vineyards of Timnah. Now to his surprise, a young lion came roaring against him. And the Spirit of the LORD came mightily upon him, and he tore the lion apart as one would have torn apart a young goat, though he had nothing in his hand. But he did not tell his father or his mother what he had done* (Judges 14:5–6).

God's strength was poured into Samson again as he carried the gates of Gaza to the top of the hill (see Judges 16:1–3). God's strength was poured into Samson one final time as he brought the temple crumbling down upon himself and the 3,000 people watching (see Judges 16:28–30).

You might think that God's power is only poured into great men with the strength of Samson but consider this: there was a bush in the wilderness. A completely worthless bush that served no real purpose. A non-entity. Yet God poured His power into that bush and it caught on fire just as a shepherd named Moses was walking by. God spoke to Moses out of that bush. He called Moses to deliver Israel out of slavery. The course of human history was forever changed by a worthless bush (see Exodus 3:1–4)!

Do you see yourself as the equivalent of a bush? You may not be among the giant sequoias and redwood trees of California, you may not have the strength of Samson, but could you at least be among the bushes? If so, then rise up—do great things in the name of the Lord Jesus Christ! You have the power of the Holy Ghost within you to change the course of history, but you'll never do it wasting your life away because you think you can't make a difference being a bush. Start proclaiming God's promises. Let me hear you say, "Why not me? If God is God, and the Word of God is true, why not me?!" God is waiting to find the man, the woman, the church, the nation, who will trust Him with ALL their heart. That is where He will pour out His power.

PRAYER

God, I trust You with my whole heart. I believe that ordinary becomes extraordinary when Your power is poured out. With Your power at work in my life, NOTHING is impossible! When others ask, "Why you?" I will answer, "Why not me?!" In Jesus' name; Amen.

WISDOM OF THE WORD

63

All Scripture is given by inspiration of God, and is profitable for doctrine, for reproof, for correction, for instruction in righteousness, that the man of God may be complete, thoroughly equipped for every good work.

2 TIMOTHY 3:16–17

The Bible does not begin in Matthew, with the birth of Jesus; it begins at Genesis with the creation of the universe: "In the beginning, God created the heavens and the earth" (Genesis 1:1). The word of God was there, in Genesis 1:1, and from the very beginning:

> *In the beginning was the Word, and the Word was with God, and the Word was God. He was in the beginning with God. All things were made through Him, and without Him nothing was made that was made. In Him was life, and the life was the light of men. And the light shines in the darkness, and the darkness did not comprehend it* (John 1:1–5).

The Bible is authored by the Holy Spirit; it is "God-breathed" (2 Timothy 3:16 NIV). It is infallible. It is inerrant. It is the everlasting Word of God. It is the moral foundation of civilization. Wisdom and instruction come from the Word of God, and you are wise to heed it: "The fear of the LORD is the beginning of knowledge, but fools despise wisdom and instruction" (Proverbs 1:7).

The Bible is greater than other books, as the Rocky Mountains are greater than a single grain of sand. The Bible is greater than other books, as the blazing sun at high noon is greater than the glow of a candle on a child's birthday cake. The Bible is greater than other books, as the seven seas of the earth are greater than the dripping faucet in your kitchen. The Bible is not just a "good" book; the Bible is the *only* Book.

The Bible is a lamp unto my feet and a light unto my path. You don't read the Bible; the Bible reads you. The Bible is sharper than a two-edged sword. It divides the truth from a lie, right from wrong, light from darkness. The Bible is the moral compass of the soul. It is the truth, the whole truth, and nothing but the truth. The Word of God is a treasure chest of unsearchable riches. This is the Word of the Living God.

> But you must continue in the things which you have learned and been assured of, knowing from whom you have learned them, and that from childhood you have known the Holy Scriptures, which are able to make you wise for salvation through faith which is in Christ Jesus (2 Timothy 3:14–15).

Live it, love it, read it, keep at it. Know the Word and the One who authored it: this is your Source; this is your Truth; this is the Guide that shows you right from wrong. Pity the fool who despises the wisdom of the Word.

PRAYER

Father, I believe that You are the author of wisdom and instruction. And, Your Word is not a good book, it is THE Good Book! Daily, I commit to reading Your Word and to allowing it to guide, convict, correct, instruct, train, and teach me to walk in Your ways. In Jesus' name; Amen!

WHAT ARE YOU LOOKING FOR?

64

When Jesus turned and saw them following, he said to them, "What are you looking for?" They said to him, "Rabbi."

JOHN 1:38 NRSV

Imagine that it was you following Jesus. When He turned and looked you in the eye and asked: "What are you looking for?"—how would you answer?

Are you looking for a friend?

God is a friend that sticks closer than a brother (see Proverbs 18:24). If your father and mother forsake you, God will pick you up (see Psalm 27:10).

Are you looking for something to put your hope in?

David said, God is "my glory and the One who lifts up my head" (Psalm 3:3). He said, "Why are you cast down, O my soul? And why are you disquieted within me? Hope in God; for I shall yet praise Him, the help of my countenance and my God" (Psalm 42:11). David said, "You are my hiding place and my shield; I hope in Your word" (Psalm 119:114) and "now, Lord, what do I wait for? My hope is in You" (Psalm 39:7).

Are you looking for joy unspeakable?

The Bible says, "Do not sorrow, for the joy of the LORD is your strength" (Nehemiah 8:10). "In Your presence is fullness of joy" (Psalm 16:11). "Weeping may endure for a night, but joy comes in the morning" (Psalm 30:5). "Make a joyful shout to the LORD, all you lands! Serve the LORD with gladness; come before His presence with singing" (Psalm 100:1–2).

Are you looking for health and healing?

When Jesus was on the earth, He healed one-on-one. He also healed in mass. And when He went to the Cross, He healed once and for all: "... by His stripes we are healed" (Isaiah 53:5). He is *Jehovah Rapha*, "the LORD who heals you" (Exodus 15:26). Jesus is still the Great Physician for whatever affliction you face today.

There is no God but the God of Abraham, Isaac, and Jacob. There is no answer but the answer that comes through Jesus Christ. There is no hope but from the God of all hope. Therefore, we can come before the throne to be healed, lifted up, restored, and reenergized, to look into the future and know that everything is going to be all right because God is with us and He is for us. Whatever you are looking for, the answer can be found in Him. Give God praise!

PRAYER

God, I believe that no matter what the question is, no matter what I am looking for, the answer is in Jesus Christ, my Lord! Jesus, You are my best friend, my light in the darkness, hope in my sorrows, my health and healing. You are joy unspeakable. I receive divine health for my life and those I love. I receive Your exceedingly great joy. I will walk in Your light and not stumble. Everything that has been taken from me has been restored. You are my all in all! In Jesus' name; Amen.

YET, I WILL BE CONFIDENT

65

The LORD is my light and my salvation— whom shall I fear? The LORD is the stronghold of my life— of whom shall I be afraid? When the wicked advance against me to devour me, it is my enemies and foes who will stumble and fall. Though an army besiege me, my heart will not fear; though war break out against me, even then I will be confident.

PSALM 27:1–3 NIV

It's a fact that Americans are losing confidence in themselves and they're losing confidence in our future as a nation. People are leaving America in search of a new home, fleeing the chaos in the streets, in our federal government, in our public schools.

That lack of confidence will destroy your peace of mind. A lack of confidence can destroy your marriage, your hopes for your children, your physical health. A lack of confidence will assassinate every opportunity that comes to you. A lack of confidence crushes your dreams before you ever have them. A lack of confidence makes you see the dark side of every issue that comes in contact with you. You will never accomplish your divine destiny until you crucify the insecurity that haunts you night and day, and begin to say, "even then I will be confident."

As Joshua was preparing to lead the Israelites across the Jordan River and into the Promised Land, God literally *commanded* him to have divine confidence (see Joshua 1:9). Moses had just died. Joshua had tried once before to convince the Israelites to enter the Promised Land and they had threatened to stone him (see Numbers 14:10). He knew very well that there were giants in the land that could overtake them. It was precisely for these reasons that God *commanded* Joshua: "Be strong and courageous. Do not be afraid; do not be discouraged, for the LORD your God will be with you wherever you go" (Joshua 1:9 NIV).

What about you? Do you need to be reminded

that God is with you wherever you go? Do you need to be *commanded* not to fear or be discouraged? Do you need a confidence boost when it comes to your future, your career, your friends, your family, your nation, even yourself? I want you, today, to experience an explosion of divine confidence that will allow you to live a life of continuous adventure, embracing all that God has for you. In the words of the Apostle Paul, "... being confident of this, that he who began a good work in you will carry it on to completion until the day of Jesus Christ" (Philippians 1:6 NIV). Believe in God. Believe in yourself. Believe in others. Embrace the divine confidence that comes from God!

PRAYER

Father God, today in the authority of Jesus' name, let divine and supernatural confidence explode in my heart and mind. The confidence I have is not based on a world system; it is based on Your Word. I am a child of You, the Most High God. I am established on the solid rock of Christ that is eternal and unshakeable. In Jesus' name; Amen!

FROM LITTLE FAITH TO GREAT FAITH

66

When Jesus heard it, He marveled, and said to those who followed, "Assuredly, I say to you, I have not found such great faith, not even in Israel!"

MATTHEW 8:10

The Gospel of Matthew records several instances when Jesus talks about the "little faith" and "great faith" of the people. The disciples had "little faith" when the storm hit in Matthew 8 and Jesus was asleep in the boat. They thought Jesus was going to let them drown, not caring enough to get up from His nap. Fast forward to another storm in Matthew 14, as Jesus walked on water toward the disciples. Peter stepped out of the boat, seemingly buoyed by faith, only to begin to sink the moment he took his eyes off Jesus. Jesus reached out to save him, saying, "O you of little faith, why did you doubt?" (v. 31).

Jesus talks to the crowd from the Mount of Olives in Matthew 6, about their "little faith" that causes them to worry about what they will eat, drink, and wear. He says, "Wherefore, if God so clothe the grass of the field, which today is, and tomorrow is cast into the oven, shall he not much more clothe you, O ye of little faith?" (Matthew 6:30 KJV).

But Jesus doesn't just talk about the "little faith" of the people. He also points out when they have "great faith." In Matthew 8, a centurion approaches Jesus, asking him to heal his servant. Jesus offers to go with the centurion, but the centurion says:

> *"Lord, I am not worthy that You should come under my roof. But only speak a word, and my servant will be healed. For I also am a man under authority, having soldiers under me. And I say to this one, 'Go,' and he goes; and to*

another, 'Come,' and he comes; and to my servant, 'Do this,' and he does it" (Matthew 8:8–9).

Jesus responds by saying He has "not found such great faith, not even in Israel" (v. 10). He tells the centurion to head home, where he'll find his servant healed: "as you have believed, so let it be done for you" (v. 13).

Similarly, an account in Matthew 15 tells of a Gentile woman who comes to Jesus because her daughter is demon-possessed. The disciples try to send her away, and even Jesus tells her that the Jews are His priority. She pleads with Him, determined to see her daughter healed. Her argument: "'even the little dogs eat the crumbs which fall from their masters' table'" (v. 27). To which Jesus responds: "'O woman, great is your faith! Let it be to you as you desire.' And her daughter was healed from that very hour" (v. 28).

How do you get from little faith to great faith? By fighting the good fight. By fighting one fight, and then another that is bigger than that fight, and then another, and another. The battles you are in continuously increase in size until you are fighting giants. That's what great faith is.

PRAYER

Lord, I believe that my stumbling blocks will become my stepping stones. I am determined to see every opposition as an opportunity to grow from little faith to great faith. I will fight the good fight. I will finish the race! In Jesus' name; Amen.

BY FAITH

67

"Now the just shall live by faith; but if anyone draws back, my soul has no pleasure in him."

HEBREWS 10:38

What does it mean to live "by faith"? In order to understand faith, it is important to understand confidence. Confidence is made up of two words: *con* meaning "with," and *faido* meaning "faith." Confidence means living with faith. So, to live by faith is to live with confidence—assurance, trust, coolness under pressure—knowing that God is who He says He is, and He will do what He says He will do.

Scripture gives us countless examples of what it looks like to live by faith.

By faith, Elijah didn't die, but was translated into heaven in a chariot of fire (see 2 Kings 2:11).

By faith, Noah built an ark in a world that had never seen rain (see Genesis 6 & 7). He told the people there was going to come such water that this giant boat would float! That's faith.

By faith, Abraham at 100 years of age went home to his ninety-year-old wife and told her they would be rocking a baby by that same time next year (see Genesis 17). Sarah laughed. I believe she laughed hysterically. But from her womb that was twice dead came Isaac, whose name means "the son of laughter." Nothing is impossible with God. Nothing!

By faith, Moses refused to be called the son of Pharaoh's daughter (see Exodus 2). He refused to be identified as royalty, instead identifying with the two-million slaves who were going to leave Egypt and live for 40 years in the wilderness before eventually settling in the Promised Land. Why did Moses do that? The Bible says he did it that he might "receive the crown of glory that does not fade away" (1 Peter 5:4). He saw further than this life could take him. He saw, in faith, a Kingdom that would never end when Jesus Christ sets up His throne in the city of Jerusalem.

The point: to live "by faith" means that when God says a miracle is coming, get ready for the miracle. If God sends you fishing for Moby Dick with a cane pole, take tartar sauce because you are going to catch a big fish. If God says you are going to have a baby, you better put the crib together. If God says it, it will happen. Have faith in God. When God says the answer is coming, the answer is coming. It will be there. Live in divine confidence!

You might say, "I prayed last night, and nothing has happened." Well, God doesn't run on your clock. He has His own clock. But God's delays are not God's denials. He heard you. Your miracle is coming. Rejoice! Be glad the problem is solved. You may not see it yet, but it is already done. Give God praise!

PRAYER

God, I praise You for giving me my miracle. Even though I may not see it with my natural eye, I know it's going to happen; and I praise You for it. I'm standing on Your Word and saying it will happen! In Jesus' name; Amen.

FAITH GROWS

68

So then faith comes by hearing, and hearing by the word of God.

ROMANS 10:17

Faith is not inherited, it is developed. You don't acquire faith from your parents or the people who raised you. Faith grows as you grow. Romans 10:17 says, "Faith *cometh* by hearing, and hearing by the word of God" (KJV). The word *cometh* is a Greek continuance verb, meaning faith is continuing to grow in you, predicated on your obedience to the Word of God. When you hear the Word of God and you obey it, you go from glory to glory. You grow from first to second to third grade faith. To middle school, high school, graduate school, and now you are really fighting big battles. And you're not concerned because you and God have a working relationship. Don't be bound by your own self-imposed limitations. Great faith is born on the battlefield of life. Great testimonies are the outcome of great tests. Great triumphs can only come from great trials.

In the flesh we say, "I'll believe it when I see it." But in the Spirit, we believe it before we see it because we have confidence in God. If you must see it before you can believe it, you need to develop your faith; you need to grow from one level to the next by studying and obeying the Word of God. When you stop exercising your faith, you lose your faith. Feed your faith and your doubts will starve to death. According to your faith, be it unto you. Every product in the pantry of heaven comes on the currency of faith in God.

There is faith unlimited in the Bible. The devil is not afraid of you, but when you start quoting the Bible, he becomes terrified of you. You have awesome power in the name, the blood, and in the Word of Jesus. Just as Jesus resisted Satan's temptations in the desert by quoting the Bible, you too can overcome every test, trial, temptation, and storm with "the sword of the Spirit, which is the word of God" (Ephesians 6:17).

Is faith important for your daily life? Just think about living one day without it. There are a thousand ways to please the Lord, but none of them will work without faith. Faith helps you walk fearlessly, run confidently, and live victoriously. Faith is not believing that God can do it; faith is believing that God will do it and He will do it for you, and He will do it right now. That's what faith is.

PRAYER

God, You are an awesome God. You cannot fail. You are wonderful, majestic, my Almighty Provider. You are greater than my problems, my enemies, the mountains I am trying to climb, the giants who are threatening to kill me. You are higher than the highest, greater than the greatest, wiser than the wisest. I declare that I will walk by faith in You! In Jesus' name; Amen.

WHAT FAITH CAN DO

69

But Jesus looked at them and said, "With men it is impossible, but not with God; for with God all things are possible."

MARK 10:27

Faith can help you accomplish anything. The Israelites conquered giants in the Bible. The three Hebrew young men walked in and out of the fiery furnace without the smell of smoke upon them. Moses led two million people across the wilderness for 40 years. It rained manna every morning, so they did not go hungry. They had a cloud by day to cool them off and a fire by night to keep them warm. Water gushed out of a rock, bringing nourishment to two million people and their livestock. There was not one sick nor feeble among them for 40 years. As if that weren't enough—their clothes did not wear out!

Joshua commanded the sun and moon to stand still for a day, and it did. Elijah called fire from heaven to consume the sacrifice to prove to Israel it was in a backslidden state. The sacrifice was soaked with twelve barrels of water, one for each tribe of Israel, yet fire still came from heaven and consumed it. When the archangel Gabriel came to Mary, a teenager, he said she was going to be the mother of God. Just think about that. Becoming the mother of God is a mind-expanding concept. Yet when the angel finished, Mary said, "My soul magnifies the Lord, and my spirit has rejoiced in God my Savior" (Luke 1:46–47). She was confident that everything was going to be all right.

Paul preached in chains to Felix, a Roman governor, causing the governor to tremble. Paul shook deadly vipers from his wrist on the island of Malta. The night before he was beheaded by the Roman Empire, he wrote to Timothy, "I have fought the good fight, I have finished the race,

I have kept the faith. Finally, there is laid up for me the crown of righteousness, which the Lord, the righteous Judge, will give to me on that Day, and not to me only but also to all who have loved His appearing" (2 Timothy 4:7–8). That is what faith can do.

The Bible says, the Lord is your fortress and Deliverer. He is your *Jehovah Shammah*. He is *Jehovah Jireh*. He's the God who is there. He is the rock of your salvation. He is the One who was, and is, and ever more shall be. He is the fairest of ten thousand. He is Wonderful Counselor, Mighty God, Everlasting Father. He is the Bright Morning Star, the Lily of the Valley, and the Rose of Sharon. He is the conqueror of death, hell, and the grave. He is the Lord of glory, the Light of the World, the Lamb of God, the Lion of Judah. And when your confidence is in Him, there is nothing that you cannot do.

PRAYER

Lord, faith does not demand miracles—faith produces miracles. Faith is the victory that overcomes the world. And the victory is mine in every battle, because You are by my side. I declare that there is nothing I cannot do because my faith, my confidence is in You. In Jesus' name; Amen.

WHEN YOU NEED A LITTLE UMPH

70

For You, LORD, have made me glad through Your work; I will triumph in the works of Your hands.

PSALM 92:4

"... I will *triumph* in the works of Your hands." Look at the word *triumph*. It sounds like *try-umph*, like it needs a little push, a little *umph*. So, what if you have failed before? Solomon said, "for though the righteous fall seven times, they rise again ..." (Proverbs 24:16 NIV). If you've fallen down seven times, get up. Don't lose confidence in yourself! God is still on the throne and His plan for your life can still come together.

How do you know if you've lost confidence in yourself? You know you lack confidence when you look for reasons why you can't try something new. You say things like, "It'll never work," or "I've already tried that and failed."

You know you lack confidence when you refuse to act upon solutions to your problem. You may know exactly what to do, and yet you are too afraid to do it.

You know you lack confidence when you seek out too many counselors. Let me tell you, if you consult a committee of 12, you'll get 13 different opinions and you'll be so confused you won't be able to find the doorknob. I've even heard it said that a camel is a racehorse designed by a committee of 12!

You know you lack confidence when you're fearful of responsibility. You have sentenced yourself to a life of mediocrity. You've sentenced yourself to a rut, which is just a grave with both ends kicked out. You may even turn down a promotion at work because you don't want the responsibility. To that I have only one thing to say: get off your blessed assurance and take the promotion, rise to another level, and start producing like you've never produced before! Let God reward you for daring to be different!

You know you lack confidence when the boss calls you in and your first reaction is, "What did I do wrong?" Instead, your reaction should be: "I'm getting a promotion! I'm getting a raise! I'm getting accolades through the roof for a job well done!"

Hear this: when a tiger is charging you, you have two choices—you can stand motionless and become lunch, or you can attack. If you stand motionless, your fate is certain. But if you attack, the tiger will think you are insane and run away. So, push through your fears! Give yourself a little *umph*! You are a child of God. You are sons and daughters of royalty. You are priests and kings unto God. Attack the opportunities that come your way! Dare to be different! Dare to reach the highest level!

One final word: tomorrow, some of you are going to get the opportunity to do something great that will change your life. And I promise you that the first three things you're going to feel are not happy, happy, happy, but insecurity, uncertainty, and fear. Push through that! Get on the other side of that. Give it a little umph and be who God intended you to be from the start.

PRAYER

I am confident in You, my Savior, who gives me the umph I need to dare to be different, to dare to go higher, and to dare to be all that God has called me to be! In Jesus' name; Amen.

THERE IS NO SUCH THING AS INDECISION

71

"Assuredly, I say to you, whatever you bind on earth will be bound in heaven, and whatever you loose on earth will be loosed in heaven."

MATTHEW 18:18

Scripture tells us that what we bind on earth will be bound in heaven, and what we loose on earth will be loosed in heaven. We bind and loose on earth, then God reacts in heaven. We start it, then God follows through with the power to get it done. But the initiative is ours. The ball is in our court.

I've heard people say, "I wonder when God is going to do something for me." But I think God is looking back at you and saying, "I wonder when *you're* going to do something for *yourself!*" Remember, the initiative is yours; the ball is in your court.

Granted, you won't win every game you play. You won't fascinate every person you meet. Every phone call will not be good news. But stop looking for a quick fix to your problem! You can't do everything at once, but you can do something right now. Make a decision and take action; with persistence, you will be victorious.

Former President Calvin Coolidge, 30th US President, said:

> *Nothing in this world can take the place of persistence. Talent will not; nothing is more common than unsuccessful men with talent. Genius will not; unrewarded genius is almost a proverb. Education will not; the world is full of educated derelicts. Persistence and determination alone are omnipotent. The slogan Press on! has solved and will always solve the problems of the human race.*

Be persistent. Be determined. Press on. Push forward. A temporary setback does not mean God doesn't love you. The fact that you're having trouble is living proof that you're a card-carrying member of the human race. That's all it means! How do we maintain confidence? How do we overcome those moments in life when we feel intimidated or inadequate or even defeated by the opportunity that's coming our way? Give up every thought about quitting. The Bible says, "But he who endures to the end shall be saved" (Matthew 24:13). You will never stand in the winner's circle unless you finish the race. Stopping at third base is just as bad as making an out. Never give in and never give up. Quitters do not win, and winners do not quit.

Honestly, I don't believe there is any such thing as indecision. You either decide, or you decide not to decide. You might say you haven't made up your mind, but you have. You made up your mind to do nothing. And you also have the power to make up your mind to do something. Make up your mind to achieve something that God is giving you the opportunity to do. Hang tough. Fight the good fight. Have confidence in Christ. Nothing is impossible with God. He is your Father. Victory is yours!

PRAYER

God, today I will do something. I will make a decision and take action. It might not get me all the way to my goal, but at least I'm heading in the right direction! In Jesus' name; Amen.

NO EXCUSES

72

You are of God, little children, and have overcome them, because He who is in you is greater than he who is in the world.

1 JOHN 4:4

We start developing self-confidence when we stop making excuses about our situation. All great living begins when you accept responsibility for your life. If you make excuses, no one can help you, not even God.

Look at the excuses Jesus could have used: *I can't do anything because people say I was illegitimate. I was part of the hated minority. I was born in political captivity. When I grew up, church leaders called me a heretic, a drunkard, a traitor, a liar. Judas betrayed me. Peter is cursing my memory. Thomas doubted me. I didn't even get a proper burial.*

But Jesus didn't make excuses. Jesus looked hell's legions in the eye and said, "I am the conqueror of death, hell, and the grave" (see Revelation 1:18). Paul said, "He has disarmed Satan and publicly put him to shame" (see Colossians 2:13–15). What does that mean? That means that when Jesus died on the cross, He went into hell, took Satan by the hair and drug him through the fire, parading him in front of every demon. Jesus said to Satan, "I defeated you at the cross. You are a defeated foe. And when my children come to the gate using My name, you will turn them loose because they are My victorious bride."

How many of you can say, "Pastor, I've allowed a lot of things to intimidate me in my life. I read the verse, 'Greater is He that is in me than he that is in the world,' but I still feel these feelings of insecurity and fear and have a lack of confidence." Never let those feelings make you live the inferior role! If there are areas in your life crippled by a lack of confidence, pray for God's divine confidence to invade your life today—thought life, marriage, workplace, health—whatever area where you need confidence in spades, God can give it to you right now.

There is power in the blood of Jesus. There is power in the authority of the Word of God. When you begin to speak the Word of God, under the anointing of the Holy Spirit, you can charge the gates of hell with a water pistol and be victorious. We serve a God of power, more power than the world and all its military can possibly imagine. Don't you ever forget it!

With God, you have are going to live an unconquerable future, an exciting walk where each day God takes you from one glory to another to experience His infinite grace and supernatural provision. Rejoice and be exceedingly glad, because God your Father is waiting for you to become His champion on earth.

PRAYER

Heavenly Father, in the name of Your Son Jesus Christ, I'm coming to You today asking for a baptism of righteous and powerful confidence, one that is based on Your Word, built in faith, that will not be discouraged, and that will be bold and aggressive. I'm done making excuses. I'm going forward to live the great adventure that heaven has designed for me. In Jesus' name; Amen.

JESUS' FINAL COMMAND

73

"Behold, I send the Promise of My Father upon you; but tarry in the city of Jerusalem until you are endued with power from on high."

LUKE 24:49

As Jesus was getting ready to leave the earth, He met with His disciples one last time:

> And being assembled together with them, He commanded them not to depart from Jerusalem, but to **wait** for the Promise of the Father, "which," He said, "you have heard from Me; for John truly baptized with water, but you shall be baptized with the Holy Spirit not many days from now" (Acts 1:4–5, emphasis added).

Jesus had just given them the Great Commission, telling them that they would be personally responsible for carrying His name to the ends of the earth. They must have been so energized! Jesus had risen from the dead, and now He was commissioning them to be world changers! Everything was all making sense now! They were probably chomping at the bit to get started! But Jesus' final word to them was, "wait."

I don't know anyone who likes to hear the word "wait." Small children know it is a bad word and we never grow out of feeling that way! But God had a plan for the disciples. He had a reason for asking them to wait.

Isaiah 40:31 says, "But those who *wait* on the LORD shall renew their strength ..." Noah built the ark and waited for rain. Jacob worked for his uncle for years, waiting to marry his beloved Rachel. David played his harp as a servant to Saul, waiting his turn to take the throne. Simeon and Anna waited in the temple to see the newborn Messiah. Good things come to those who wait!

Even though the disciples must have been eager to start their ministry, they obeyed Jesus' final command. They tarried there in the Upper Room. They waited. And on the tenth day, the Holy Spirit came to the Upper Room. Cloven tongues of fire sat upon the heads of the disciples and they spoke with other tongues, giving birth to the New Testament Church. They spoke 120 languages in the streets, declaring the message of salvation to the nearly two-million people who were in Jerusalem for the Passover. They were speaking in a heavenly language, and all those nations heard the Gospel. A global evangelistic explosion happened right there, because all those people heard what heaven had for them. The disciples had obeyed Jesus' command to wait, and the result was an absolute miracle!

Is there an area in your life where God is asking you to wait? Is He asking you to wait on a promotion at work? Is He asking you to wait to get married until He brings the right spouse into your life? Is He asking you to not give up on a situation, but to wait to see the goodness of the Lord? You will never have peace in your life if you run ahead of your Guide. Remember: "The Lord isn't really being slow about his promise, as some people think. No, he is being patient for your sake ... " (2 Peter 3:9 NLT). Good things come to those who wait!

PRAYER

God, Your ways are not my ways and Your timing is not my timing. You are never late to keep Your promises. I know they will show up right on time. I declare that I will eagerly wait upon You and trust that I will see Your goodness in the land of the living! In Jesus' name; Amen.

A MINISTRY OF MIRACLES

74

"Call to Me, and I will answer you, and show you great and mighty things, which you do not know."

JEREMIAH 33:3

Do you need a miracle to happen in your life? I've got great news! The Bible, from Genesis to Revelation, is one endless miracle after another.

Jesus, who we worship and adore, had a ministry based on miracles. He healed the blind, the lame, and the leper. He touched the untouchable. He forgave the unforgiveable. He turned water into wine. He turned the funeral procession for the widowed woman's son into a parade of joy because He raised that boy back to life. He healed a man by the pool of Bethesda who had been there for 38 years with one little sentence: "Rise, take up your bed, and walk" (John 5:8). He walked on the sea with the winds and waves fighting against Him, restructuring the molecular power of water since He created it to begin with. It was the voice of the Creator [Jesus] speaking to the created [water]: "I need to walk on you; be still." He shouted to Lazarus, "Come forth," and the dead man walked out of his grave into the arms of his sisters (see John 11:43). He fed thousands from a boy's sack lunch. He was crucified at Calvary and on the third day walked out of His grave just like He said He would.

Throughout Jesus' ministry on earth, He healed with a word, a touch, a command, His compassion. He even healed with His spit. One story is told in Mark 8:22–25,

> *Then He came to Bethsaida; and they brought a blind man to Him, and begged Him to touch him. So He took the blind man by the hand and led him*

out of the town. And when He had spit on his eyes and put His hands on him, He asked him if he saw anything. And he looked up and said, "I see men like trees, walking." Then He put His hands on his eyes again and made him look up. And he was restored and saw everyone clearly."

And another in John 9:6–7,

When He had said these things, He spat on the ground and made clay with the saliva; and He anointed the eyes of the blind man with the clay. And He said to him, "Go, wash in the pool of Siloam" (which is translated, Sent). So he went and washed, and came back seeing.

Why did Jesus use His spit to heal these men? Because the Jewish people believed there was healing power in the saliva of a firstborn son. Jesus spit into His hand and put the dirt there and massaged that together and put it in the eyes of the blind man as a witness to every Jewish person that He was the Firstborn Son of God the Father, who had absolute healing power for the nations of the world.

You don't have to seek miracles; seek Jesus. You too can walk in the supernatural and receive miracles from God on a regular basis when you follow Him.

PRAYER

I believe in the miracle-working power of You, Jesus.

HOLY COMMUNION

75

For I received from the Lord that which I also delivered to you: that the Lord Jesus on the same night in which He was betrayed took bread; and when He had given thanks, He broke it and said, "Take, eat; this is My body which is broken for you; do this in remembrance of Me. In the same manner He also took the cup after supper, saying, "This cup is the new covenant in My blood. This do, as often as you drink it, in remembrance of Me." For as often as you eat this bread and drink this cup, you proclaim the Lord's death till He comes.

1 CORINTHIANS 11:23–26

The Holy Communion is an illustrated sermon in two parts. First, it looks back to the death of Christ on the Cross, and second, it looks forward to the second coming of Jesus.

Everything of significance in the Bible begins and ends with the Cross. Paul said that without the shedding of the blood on the Cross, there is no remission of sin: "And according to the law almost all things are purified with blood, and without shedding of blood there is no remission" (Hebrews 9:22).

The blood covenant is what makes it possible for us to be here today. The devil is not afraid of you, but he is terrified of the blood. Communion is a reminder about the power of the blood: "For this is My blood of the new covenant, which is shed for many for the remission of sins" (Matthew 26:28). We would all be captives and slaves to sin and Satan without the blood of Jesus. The power in the blood is a message we all need to hear. He was wounded for our transgressions, and by His stripes we are healed.

The Holy Communion looks back to the death of Christ, but it also looks forward to the Second Coming of Jesus Christ as King of kings and Lord of lords, when He will establish His Kingdom on the earth that shall never pass away. Jesus said in Matthew 26:29, "But I say to you, I will not drink of this fruit of the vine from now on until that day when I drink it new with you in My Father's kingdom." Very soon the trumpet of God is going to sound. The dead in Christ are going to rise. And we, who are living, shall be caught up to be with the Lord in the air.

> For the Lord Himself will descend from heaven with a shout, with the voice of an archangel, and with the trumpet of God. And the dead in Christ will rise first. Then we who are alive and remain shall be caught up together with them in the clouds to meet the Lord in the air. And thus we shall always be with the Lord (1 Thessalonians 4:16–17).

The Holy Communion was God's direct revelation to Paul for the church. Paul writes: "For I received from the Lord that which I also delivered to you ..." (1 Corinthians 11:23). Paul was saying, I didn't make this up. I'm telling you what heaven told me.

PRAYER

Jesus, thank You for shedding Your blood, the blood that takes away my sins. I declare my sole allegiance to You and look forward to the soon and coming Kingdom that will never end. To God be the glory! In Your name I pray; Amen.

GIVE THANKS

76

In everything give thanks; for this is the will of God in Christ Jesus for you.

1 THESSALONIANS 5:8

Let me set the scene: Jesus is in the Upper Room with His disciples, sharing in the Last Supper. He was moments away from being betrayed by the kiss of Judas. He was moments away from being denied by Peter and abandoned by the others. The shadow of the Cross hung over Him. He was about to be crucified as a criminal by masters of brutality. Yet Jesus gave thanks (see 1 Corinthians 11:24). He gave thanks!

This was not uncommon for Jesus. In fact, this was His signature move. When He broke bread with His disciples, He gave thanks. Before He fed the 5,000, He gave thanks. He gave thanks standing outside Lazarus' tomb. He gave thanks the night that Judas betrayed Him, and Peter denied Him. Jesus gave thanks in ordinary circumstances, at a picnic and amongst friends. Jesus gave thanks in troubling circumstances, at the death of a beloved friend and in His own final hours. And God turned those ordinary, troubling circumstances into extraordinary encounters.

Jesus gave thanks for the five loaves and two fish and all 5,000 men and their companions were fed to satisfaction, with 12 baskets full of leftovers (see Matthew 14:19–21). Jesus gave thanks outside Lazarus's tomb, "And he who had died came out bound hand and foot with grave clothes" (John 11:44), to the glory of God. Jesus gave thanks as He shared the Holy Communion with His disciples, giving Him the strength to go to the Cross with these words: "not My will, but Yours, be done" (Luke 22:42).

What can we learn from this? The spirit of thanksgiving is what releases the miracle-working power of God!

Don't go to God whining, pining, and complaining. Thank the Lord! Exalt the Lord! Praise Him in your deepest, darkest valley. And as you do, you will begin to walk out of those valleys into the sunshine of God's love. The thunderclap of heaven will go off and supernatural things will begin to happen!

Over and over the psalmist writes: "Oh, give thanks to the LORD, for He is good! For His mercy endures forever" (Psalm 107:1). Are you going through a raging storm? Are you in a personal crisis? Have your dearest friends betrayed you? Be thankful to Him and bless His name, for the Lord is good and His mercy endures forever. Find yourself a place to pray and begin to rejoice at the good things heaven is doing. In everything, give thanks!

PRAYER

Thanks be unto You, Father, for Your mercy, grace, and love. You are the Light in my darkest hour. You are the Strength in my weakness. You are Good, even when nothing seems to be going my way. I declare that I will give thanks with a grateful heart in all circumstances, trusting You to work all things together for good under heaven. In Jesus' name; Amen.

THE MARRIAGE SUPPER

77

For as often as you eat this bread and drink this cup, you proclaim the Lord's death till He comes.

1 CORINTHIANS 11:26

The Holy Communion is a memorial meal celebrating Christ's victory over the Cross for you. Victory over death, hell, and the grave. Satan is a defeated foe; the prince of darkness was crushed at the Cross. He cannot touch you. He cannot harm you. He cannot control you. He cannot manipulate you. The victory is yours in Jesus Christ! Christ's death and resurrection guarantees that you are going to come out of your grave on resurrection morning.

Jesus' victory over death, hell, and the grave, guaranteed that there is a place called heaven. It's a very real place and it's just one heartbeat away from the righteous. In 1 Samuel 20:3, David says, "there is but a step between me and death." Just one step. My grandmother Swick was 88 years old, laying on her death bed in a coma, with my mother at her side praying, when suddenly my grandmother opened her eyes and said, "Vada, stop praying for me! I'm almost there but every time you start praying, I start coming back!" She closed her eyes and went to heaven. That's a true story! You can't get to heaven without dying, friends. Death is not something to be afraid of, because it leads us to victory.

The Holy Communion was not just something Jesus did with the 12 disciples. He commands us, as His disciples, to continue this celebration. How long are we to celebrate the Holy Communion? Until He comes (see 1 Corinthians 11:26). What happens if you go to heaven before He returns? You'll celebrate the Holy Communion there too! In heaven we are going to celebrate the

Holy Communion around the marriage supper. We'll cast our crowns at His feet. The communion declares that He is the Living Savior. His name is Jesus, Lamb of God, Lord of Glory. He is *Emmanuel*, "God With Us," the hope of glory, the great Shepherd of the Church, the great Physician who heals the sick, the King of glory; and He's coming back! Hallelujah!

We are going to sit around the marriage supper of the Lamb of God and for seven years we will rejoice and be exceedingly glad as we receive the rewards of the righteous. We will cast our crowns at His feet. At the end of seven years, mounted on white horses we, along with King Jesus, are going to descend to the city of Jerusalem. He will set up a Kingdom there, an eternal Kingdom, and of His Kingdom shall have no end. The lion will lay down with the lamb. Men will beat their swords into plowshares and study war no more. We are going to have peace, absolute peace, from that moment on. It may be a madhouse now, but God is coming down with a Kingdom of total peace, total love, total joy. Give Him praise!

PRAYER

In Your name I am not afraid of death. Death has no hold on me. Each time I partake of the Holy Communion I am celebrating Your victory over death that secured a place in heaven for me. One day I will be at the marriage supper with You, the Lamb! In Jesus' name; Amen.

IN REMEMBRANCE OF ME

78

And He took bread, gave thanks and broke it, and gave it to them, saying, "This is My body which is given for you; do this in remembrance of Me."

LUKE 22:19

When Jesus tells us to receive the Holy Communion "in remembrance of Me," what do you think He is telling us to remember?

Remember the night in Gethsemane. Remember the Roman soldiers who came to the Mount of Olives. Remember Judas' kiss. Remember Jesus' acts of righteousness. Remember the Roman whip that cut Him 39 times for your healing. Remember His blood that was shed at Calvary.

But He was wounded for our transgressions, He was bruised for our iniquities; the chastisement for our peace was upon Him, and by His stripes we are healed (Isaiah 53:5).

Remember the promise that Jesus made to you, that He would never leave you nor forsake you even to the ends of the world (see Hebrews 13:5). Remember His promise that when two or three of you gather together in His name, He is there (see Matthew 18:20). Remember, all you have to do is "'Ask, and it will be given to you; seek, and you will find; knock, and it will be opened to you'" (Matthew 7:7). Remember that God is for you, and you don't even have to think about others being against you (see Romans 8:31). Remember that you are more than a conqueror (see Romans 8:37). Remember that nothing can separate you from the love that is in Christ Jesus:

For I am persuaded that neither death nor life, nor angels nor principalities nor powers, nor things present nor things to come, nor height nor depth, nor any other created thing, shall be able to separate us from the love of God which is in Christ Jesus our Lord (Romans 8:38–39).

Remember, He is the Way-maker. He is the Burden-bearer. He is the first and the last. He is the King of kings and Lord of lords. He's your help in times of trouble. He is "the Way, the Truth, the Life" (John 14:16). He is your Deliverer. He is your Provider. He is your Healer. He is your Redeemer. He is your soon and coming King.

> ... and when He had given thanks, He broke it and said, "Take, eat; this is My body which is broken for you; do this **in remembrance of Me**." In the same manner He also took the cup after supper, saying, "This cup is the new covenant in My blood. This do, as often as you drink it, **in remembrance of Me**." For as often as you eat this bread and drink this cup, you proclaim the Lord's death till He comes (1 Corinthians 11:24–26, emphasis added).

When you receive the Holy Communion, remember that His body was broken and His blood was shed at Calvary for all mankind—that's you, that's me, that's your children, your children's children, and each generation until Christ's return. When you are in life's storms, remember. When you can't imagine a way out, remember. When life seems unbearable, remember. Remember what He has done for you. Remember who He is to you. *Remember.*

PRAYER

Lord, I remember. I remember it all. I remember who You are and what You have done. I remember. In Jesus' name; Amen.

WE ARE ONE CHURCH

79

There is one body and one Spirit, just as you were called in one hope of your calling; one Lord, one faith, one baptism; one God and Father of all, who is above all, and through all, and in you all.

EPHESIANS 4:4–6

In the theater of your mind, put yourself in the Upper Room 2,000 years ago. You're reclining on couches with the 12 disciples. Jesus is serving you with a common cup, brimming with wine. Jesus extends the goblet to you, and you see His reflection in the drink. Hear me: when you're close enough to see Jesus, impossibilities become possible and miracles are just one question away. Ask and it's yours (see Mark 11:24)!

You not only see Jesus' reflection, but you see the reflection of all the disciples in that cup. The Lord's Supper in the Upper Room describes the unity of the Church. We are one body. We have one baptism. We have one faith. We are one church, the Church of Jesus Christ.

Paul challenges all believers to make every effort "to keep the unity of the Spirit in the bond of peace" (Ephesians 4:3). Peace binds us to one another. When you partake in the Holy Communion, you are saying, "I am unified with every believer in my home. I am unified with every follower in this city. I am unified with every believer on planet earth. We are the Kingdom of God."

Romans 16:17 says, "Now I urge you, brethren, note those who cause divisions and offenses, contrary to the doctrine which you learned, and avoid them." Avoid the troublemakers. Avoid the unbelievers. Keep away from those who want to intentionally make others trip and fall. Reject those who are divisive. Keep the unity. Keep the peace. Keep participating in the Holy Communion.

But now you yourselves are to put off all these: anger, wrath, malice, blasphemy, filthy language out of your mouth. Do not lie to one another, since you have put off the old man with his deeds, and have put on the new man who is renewed in knowledge according to the image of Him who created him, where there is neither Greek nor Jew, circumcised nor uncircumcised, barbarian, Scythian, slave nor free, but Christ is all and in all (Colossians 3:8–11).

The Holy Communion conquers racism, sexism, materialism, and denominationalism. Whether you are Jew or Gentile, Greek or barbarian, master or slave, prince or pauper, white, black, or brown, American or European, Baptist or Catholic, Presbyterian or Pentecostal, male or female, we are all one in Christ Jesus.

PRAYER

Lord, I make this my declaration: there is one body; there is one church; there is one faith; there is one baptism; and You are the one God, the Godhead, Three in One. I will seek to keep the peace, to ensure unity in the church of believers. In Jesus' name; Amen.

THE CUP OF THE COVENANT

80

Likewise He also took the cup after supper, saying, "This cup is the new covenant in My blood, which is shed for you."

LUKE 22:20

God does nothing without covenant. Every flower that grows in the Word of God, grows in the soil of covenant. The Old Testament is the first covenant. The Tree of Life was God's covenant to Adam and Eve in the Garden of Eden. The rainbow was God's sign to Noah's generation that He would not destroy the earth by flood again. Every time you see a rainbow in the sky, it is a reminder of God's covenant.

And God said: "This is the sign of the covenant which I make between Me and you, and every living creature that is with you, for perpetual generations: I set My rainbow in the cloud, and it shall be for the sign of the covenant between Me and the earth. It shall be, when I bring a cloud over the earth, that the rainbow shall be seen in the cloud; and I will remember My covenant which is between Me and you and every living creature of all flesh; the waters shall never again become a flood to destroy all flesh. The rainbow shall be in the cloud, and I will look on it to remember the everlasting covenant between God and every living creature of all flesh that is on the earth." And God said to Noah, "This is the sign of the covenant which I have established between Me and all flesh that is on the earth" (Genesis 9:12–17).

God called to Abraham and He gave the Jewish people a sign. It was through circumcision that they gained entrance into the covenant with God and possessed the Promised Land. The Jewish people do not "occupy" the land of Israel; they *own* it. It has been given to them by God in covenant and Jerusalem is the eternal capital of the land of Israel.

> *This is My covenant which you shall keep, between Me and you and your descendants after you: Every male child among you shall be circumcised; and you shall be circumcised in the flesh of your foreskins, and it shall be a sign of the covenant between Me and you* (Genesis 17:10–11).

The New Testament is the second covenant. God has given to every dispensation a sign. Holy Communion is the sign and the seal of the covenant. Jesus said to His disciples, "For this is My blood of the new covenant, which is shed for many for the remission of sins" (Matthew 26:28). The communion promises the presence of Christ. When you're at His table, when you receive bread from His hand, when you hear His voice, saying, "Lo, I am with you always, even to the ends of the age" (Matthew 28:20), when you feel His touch that comforts the brokenhearted, turns darkness into glorious light, lifts the heaviest burden, transforms fears into victorious faith, and brings joy unspeakable, full of glory, you are experiencing the cup of the covenant. When you partake of the Holy Communion, you can feel the brush of angels' wings and the touch of the Master's hand, and know that, in Him, nothing is impossible to you. When you receive the Holy Communion, He is there with you. Reach out and touch Him as He goes by!

PRAYER

Lord, thank You that when I receive the cup of the covenant, I will remember that to each dispensation You have given a sign, a sign that You are with me and for me. And Your covenant will last for all generations. In Jesus' name; Amen.

A POWERFUL PLACE

81

Then the word of the LORD came to him, saying, "Arise, go to Zarephath, which belongs to Sidon, and dwell there. See, I have commanded a widow there to provide for you."

1 KINGS 17:8–9

Do you know God's purpose for your life? Have you received His power through the Holy Spirit? When you know God's purpose, and feel Him supernaturally working through your life, you'll know you are in a powerful place. In that place—God's place—is where miracles happen!

First Kings 17 tells of a great drought in all of Israel. People and animals were all starving to death, because there was no rain to nourish the crops or the animals. God said to Elijah, "Get away from here and turn eastward, and hide by the Brook Cherith, which flows into the Jordan. And it will be that you shall drink from the brook, and I have commanded the ravens to feed you *there*" (vv. 3–4, emphasis added). Elijah went where God directed him to go, and he had all the food and water he needed, just as God had said. After a time, however, the brook began to dry up because there continued to be no rain. So, God said to Elijah, "Arise, go to Zarephath, which belongs to Sidon, and dwell *there*. See, I have commanded a widow there to provide for you" (v. 9, emphasis added). Notice in both instances that God did not say go *somewhere* and be nourished. He said, go *there*—go to the place I have commanded you to go. Had Elijah gone to a different watering hole, a different town, or even the house next door, he would have starved. But he went to the brook and then to the house of the widow woman as God instructed.

When Elijah arrived at the widow's house, he asked for a drink. She agreed to give it to him and turned to go inside. Then, considering his hunger, Elijah called out, "and a morsel of bread" (v. 11). The widow only had a morsel left. Just a bit of flour and olive oil that she was going to knead together to make a last meal for herself and her son. But don't pity this woman! She was perfectly positioned for a miracle.

The truth is, everyone wants a miracle, but no one wants to be in a position that demands the miracle. However, if the place you find yourself in requires a miracle of mega proportions, hold on to your hats because God's purpose and power are about to unite!

The moment the widow of Zarephath agreed to give Elijah the last thing she had in the house, a miracle began to happen. Her bin of flour began replenishing itself and her jar of oil was on autofill. It was a double-barreled miracle that lasted for the duration of the famine. Why? How? Because Elijah was in the place God told him to be in.

The place God puts you is where God will turn up miracle power for you. Are you in the place God has put you? When you are there, you will receive His power. Big problems need big miracles, but the good news is that the God we serve is a God of miracles!

PRAYER

God of Miracles, position me to receive Your miracle-working power. I want Your purpose for my life and trust Your provision for the moment when I am in perfect position for my miracle! In Jesus' name; Amen.

THE MEAL THAT HEALS

82

"I am the living bread which came down from heaven. If anyone eats of this bread, he will live forever; and the bread that I shall give is My flesh, which I shall give for the life of the world."

JOHN 6:51

The Holy Communion is the meal that provides total healing to you: body, mind, and spirit. When you drink the cup of the Holy Communion and you eat the bread, you are drinking and eating to yourself: (1) divine health (body), (2) emotional healing (mind), and the (3) forgiveness of your sins (spirit).

The first healing of communion is divine health—a physical healing in your **body**. The history of the Holy Communion begins in the Passover. Always in the Bible, the past predicts the future and the future confirms the past.

> *And they shall take some of the blood and put it on the two doorposts and on the lintel of the houses where they eat it. Then they shall eat the flesh on that night; roasted in fire, with unleavened bread and with bitter herbs they shall eat it* (Exodus 12:7–8).

There were two parts to divine health in your body: First, the lamb's blood brought supernatural protection against the death angel that was sweeping through Egypt. Every house that did not have blood over the doorposts, the firstborn in that family died. And second, the slain lamb was to be eaten, including the main organs of the lamb's body. Think about that. Just as the lamb's blood brought protection from death, eating the lamb's body brought to the children of Israel supernatural health for the next 40 years (see Psalm 105:37). The next morning the entire nation of Israel, almost two-million slaves, came out of Egypt, saved *and* healed.

The second healing of the communion is emotional healing of our griefs and our sorrows, that is the healing in your **mind**. Isaiah 53:4 says, "Surely He has borne our griefs and carried our sorrows ..." Satan sends seven deadly emotions to try to destroy you: resentment, bitterness, unforgiveness, fear of the future, guilt of the past, grief over the loss of a loved one that lingers endlessly, and insecurity about yourself. If Satan is currently using one of these seven deadly emotions against you, receive the meal that heals.

The third healing of the communion is forgiveness of sins, that is the healing of your **spirit**. Isaiah 53:5 says, "But He was wounded for our transgressions, He was bruised for our iniquities; the chastisement for our peace was upon Him, and by His stripes we are healed." Transgressions are the sins we unknowingly commit, and iniquities are those that we commit with full knowledge that what we are doing is wrong. God put both kinds of sin on His Son Jesus, who took them to the Cross and left them there, never to be remembered any more. Your relatives may try to dredge up the past, but God won't. When you confess your sins, receiving the Holy Communion, you're as pure as the blood of Jesus can make you—whiter than snow.

The Holy Communion is the meal that heals. Communion holds the key to walking in supernatural health and deliverance for your body, mind, and spirit.

PRAYER

God, I believe that the Holy Communion is the meal that heals. When I receive the cup of the communion, I receive with it the gift You have given me of supernatural health in my body, mind, and spirit. In Jesus' name; Amen.

EXAMINE YOURSELF

83

*Therefore whoever
eats this bread
or drinks this cup
of the Lord in an
unworthy manner
will be guilty of the
body and blood of
the Lord. But let
a man examine
himself, and so let
him eat of the bread
and drink of the cup.
For he who eats and
drinks in an unwor-
thy manner eats and
drinks judgment to
himself, not discern-
ing the Lord's body.
For this reason
many are weak and
sick among you, and
many sleep. For if
we would judge our-
selves, we would not
be judged. But when
we are judged, we
are chastened by the
Lord, that we may
not be condemned
with the world.*

1 CORINTHIANS 11:27–32

The Holy Communion taken unworthily will kill you. Paul said, "For this reason many are weak and sick among you, and many sleep [in death]" (1 Corinthians 11:30). Paul was saying to the Corinthian church: some of you are partaking of the communion in a state of open sin, so God is taking your life. The communion is a very serious matter with God. It has supernatural power.

I asked my mother, when she was in her early 90s, "What do you attribute to your good health?" She said, "The Holy Communion." Years after she couldn't drive, she would call a friend or hire a taxi, so that she could be at church to receive the Holy Communion. She said, "There's healing power in that communion."

Because it is so powerful, receiving the Holy Communion in the eyes of God is very serious stuff. As you partake of the Holy Communion, examine your life to see if you're of the faith. Ask yourself these three questions.

First: "Am I obeying the Word and the will of God?" Be honest with yourself! This is a life or death matter and not to be taken lightly.

Second: "Is there hidden sin in my life?" Ask the Holy Spirit to reveal to you any places where sin might by hiding. "But God has revealed them to us through His Spirit. For the Spirit searches all things, yes, the deep things of God. For what man knows the things of a man except the spirit of the man which is in him?" (1 Corinthians 2:10–11). If the Holy Spirit reveals to you that there is hidden sin in your life, take it to the Cross immediately, before partaking in the Holy Communion, so that you may receive forgiveness and approach the Lord's Supper with a free conscience.

And third: "Am I in a proper relationship with the body of Christ?" Are you meeting together with other believers, in church and Bible study, to be an encouragement to one another (see Hebrews 10:25)? Have you forgiven others and let go of the things you hold against them (see Mark 11:25)?

If you can answer in the affirmative that you are obeying the Word and the will of God, if you are clear that there is no hidden sin in your life, and if you believe that you are in a proper relationship with the body of Christ, then come boldly before the throne of grace and receive the meal that heals!

PRAYER

Heavenly Father, in the name of the Lord Jesus Christ, I receive the Holy Communion with a clear conscience. Thank you for the forgiveness of sin. Thank you for revealing to me my areas of weakness so that I may repent of them. Give me the strength to walk in Your ways. I receive it in Jesus' name; Amen.

84

"... but if you can do anything, have pity on us and help us." And Jesus said to him, "If you can! All things are possible to him who believes." Immediately the father of the child cried out and said, "I believe; help my unbelief!"

MARK 9:22–24 RSV

The Bible is filled with impossible situations that God made possible. In Mark 9, we read about a father whose son had been possessed by a spirit since birth. He had tried everything. He had come to the end of his rope. He brought the boy to the disciples, who had been healing people left and right. But even they were not able to cast the demon out. In desperation, the father says to Jesus, "if you can do anything, have pity on us and help us" (v. 22). This was no laughing matter and yet I can't help but think Jesus chuckled, incredulous that there was any qualification to His ability as Healer.

ALL things are possible, was Jesus' response. On the wings of faith, your impossibilities become possible. Your immovable mountains will be cast into the sea. When you think there is no way—God will find a way, and He will show you the way.

Just look at the Israelites. When they were fleeing captivity, they ran right up against an impossible situation. Pharaoh's army was behind them and the Red Sea was in front of them. There was no way out. But God! God made the impossible possible by parting the waters so that they could cross on dry land.

But they weren't free yet! While the waters were parted, the Egyptian army was hot on their trail. Pharaoh led his men right through the dry channel, where waters piled high on the left and high on the right. And then another miracle happened. The book of Exodus says that God pulled the wheels of Pharaoh's chariots right off!

Now it came to pass, in the morning watch, that the LORD looked down upon the army of the Egyptians through the pillar of fire and cloud, and He troubled the army of the Egyptians. And He took off their chariot wheels, so that they drove them with difficulty; and the Egyptians said, "Let us flee from the face of Israel, for the LORD fights for them against the Egyptians" (Exodus 14:24–25).

Pharaoh's chariots didn't get stuck; God pulled their wheels right off! When God does something supernatural for you it is amazing, astounding. He will take the wheels right off the chariots of the enemies who are pursuing you. He will solve your problems. He will make a way where there is no way. He is the Lord of light and love. He has all power in heaven and on earth and He wants to show it to you. Dare to believe that the impossible is possible with God! When you fly on the wings of faith into the presence of a living God, you will experience the invasion of a divine power that makes your dreams come true.

PRAYER

Lord, You make my impossible dreams possible. You make my visions for tomorrow come true. You are my hope. ALL things are possible with You by my side. Lord, I believe; help my unbelief! In Jesus' name; Amen.

THE JEFFERSON BIBLE

85

*"Will a man rob
God? Yet you
have robbed
Me! But you say,
'In what way
have we robbed
You?' In tithes
and offerings."*

MALACHI 3:8

Did you know that Thomas Jefferson, the third president of the United States, invented his own version of the Bible? Logically enough, it is called, *The Jefferson Bible*. This is how it came to pass. In February 1804, Jefferson went to work with a razor and clipped his favorite passages out of the Bible. He clipped all the teachings of Jesus, but he excluded all the miracles. He deleted the Virgin Birth, the Resurrection, and every supernatural event in between.

Shocking? It shouldn't be. This shouldn't be shocking because we do the same thing. We may not use a razor to pick and choose the Scriptures that we will and will not obey, but we pick and choose nevertheless.

Prosperity and abundance? Yes, I want that! I want tons of that, so it stays.

Tithing? Not so much.

Healing? Absolutely!

Fasting? No thanks.

We cut out the verses of the Bible that we are too undisciplined to obey. We put Scriptures on the chopping block of human logic, and we end up with a neutered, powerless, pathetic gospel. We commit what I call "intellectual idolatry." We create God in our own image, instead of the other way around.

Malachi 3:8 says, "Will a man rob God? Yet you have robbed Me! But you say, 'In what way have we robbed You?' In tithes and offerings." In other words, anything that we withhold that belongs to God, anything of God, anything that

God commands that we choose not to obey, is stealing from Him. And God doesn't give miracles to thieves!

Jesus makes it clear in the Sermon on the Mount that breaking even one "minor" commandment is like breaking them all: "Whoever therefore breaks one of the least of these commandments, and teaches men so, shall be called least in the kingdom of heaven ..." (Matthew 5:19). Eugene Peterson's translation says it like this:

> "Trivialize even the smallest item in God's Law and you will only have trivialized yourself. But take it seriously, show the way for others, and you will find honor in the kingdom. Unless you do far better than the Pharisees in the matters of right living, you won't know the first thing about entering the kingdom" (Matthew 5:19–20 MSG).

What have you cut out of your Bible? What truth is there that you refuse to obey? Let me tell you this: you will never have the full blessing of God by picking and choosing what you will and will not obey. The Bible is either all true or it's not. You either obey it all, or you are disobedient.

PRAYER

God, I don't want half a blessing. I want the full blessing available to me through faith, believing that You are Who You say You are, and You will do what You say You will do. I don't want to be a "pick and choose" Christian. I am all in. Word-for-word. One-hundred percent Truth! In Jesus' name; Amen.

86

By faith we understand that the universe was formed at God's command, so that what is seen was not made out of what was visible.

HEBREWS 11:3 NIV

The Bible begins by presenting an Almighty God who creates the universe by His spoken word.

Then God said, "Let there be light"; and there was light (Genesis 1:3).

Then God said, "Let there be a firmament in the midst of the waters, and let it divide the waters from the waters" (Genesis 1:6).

Then God said, "Let the waters under the heavens be gathered together into one place, and let the dry land appear"; and it was so (Genesis 1:9).

Then God said, "Let the earth bring forth grass, the herb that yields seed, and the fruit tree that yields fruit according to its kind, whose seed is in itself, on the earth"; and it was so (Genesis 1:11).

Then God said, "Let there be lights in the firmament of the heavens to divide the day from the night; and let them be for signs and seasons, and for days and years and let them be for lights in the firmament of the heavens to give light on the earth"; and it was so (Genesis 1:14–15).

Then God said, "Let the waters abound with an abundance of living creatures, and let birds fly above the earth across the face of the firmament of the heavens" (Genesis 1:20).

Then God said, "Let the earth bring

forth the living creature according to its kind: cattle and creeping thing and beast of the earth, each according to its kind"; and it was so (Genesis 1:24).

Then God said, "Let Us make man in Our image, according to Our likeness; let them have dominion over the fish of the sea, over the birds of the air, and over the cattle, over all the earth and over every creeping thing that creeps on the earth" (Genesis 1:26).

He spoke, and it was so. It is very clear. Nothing happens on earth or in heaven until God says. But as His anointed representatives on the earth, we also have the right to make divine proclamations. When you proclaim Scripture, in faith believing, it has the same power and the same authority as if God Himself had spoken it. Why? Because it is His Word, not ours. We are repeating what He said.

God speaks eight times in the creation story. Eight is the number of new beginnings. When you open your mouth and speak in faith believing, God's miracle-working power will explode in your life, bringing a new beginning. Your anointed proclamation, based on the Word of God, is a supernatural power in your mouth.

PRAYER

God, You spoke the heavens and the earth into creation. You commanded the waters to separate from the land. You called the birds and animals into existence. There is super-natural power in what You say, and as a child of God You have bestowed upon me the right to make divine proclamations. There is a mira-cle in my mouth when I proclaim Your Word! In Jesus' name; Amen.

WHEN JESUS SPOKE

87

And they were astonished at His teaching, for He taught them as one having authority, and not as the scribes.

MARK 1:22

One of the many things that astonished people about Jesus—besides His healing ministry and ability to cast out demons—was that, when He taught in the synagogue, He spoke "as one having authority." He spoke as one who believed that the words of God were true. He spoke as one who believed that God had a plan and a purpose for the children of Israel. He spoke as one who believed He had the power to conquer death, hell, and the grave.

Jesus spoke to the fever in the body of Peter's mother-in-law:

> Now He arose from the synagogue and entered Simon's house. But Simon's wife's mother was sick with a high fever, and they made request of Him concerning her. So He stood over her and rebuked the fever, and it left her. And immediately she arose and served them (Luke 4:38–39).

Jesus "rebuked the fever." Eugene Peterson's translation says Jesus "told the fever to leave—and it left" (MSG). That's authority!

Jesus also spoke to the winds as He walked on the raging Sea of Galilee: "Then He arose and rebuked the wind, and said to the sea, 'Peace, be still!' And the wind ceased and there was a great calm" (Mark 4:39). The Greek translation of what He said is, "Be muzzled." He gathered the winds in His fist and shut them down with a word!

Jesus spoke to the demonic powers in the demoniac from the country of Gadarenes (see

Mark 5:1–20). He spoke to the demons and they cried out in fear, then He sent them into the herd of pigs grazing nearby. They entered the swine and ran into the sea, drowning themselves. Jesus did not interview the demons. He spoke a word and they fled. The Savior we serve is far greater than any demonic power!

When Jesus spoke, health was restored.

When Jesus spoke, raging winds grew still.

When Jesus spoke, demons fled.

When Jesus spoke, He spoke as one having authority over demons, sickness, and disease, nature, death, hell, and the grave. And He says that we, as His disciples, have the same authority in our words: "... if you *say* to this mountain, 'Be removed and be cast into the sea,' it will be done" (Matthew 21:21, emphasis added). Speak to your mountains, your sicknesses, the demons that haunt you, your past, your mistakes, your failures, your weaknesses. Speak with the authority of someone who has "been with Jesus" (Acts 4:13)!

PRAYER

Father, help me to walk in Your power and declare Your Word over every demon, every enemy that approaches me, every sickness, disease, and lack in my life. I know I have the victory because You are my Lord and King of the universe! In Jesus' name; Yes, and Amen!

GREATER THINGS

88

"Most assuredly, I say to you, he who believes in Me, the works that I do he will do also; and greater works than these he will do, because I go to My Father."

JOHN 14:12

Jesus had a miracle ministry that shook the Roman Empire. Astonishingly, He looks to you and me today in the 21st century and says, "I tell you the truth, anyone who believes in me will do the same works I have done ..." (John 14:12 NLT). Did you get that? Jesus raised the dead. He walked on water. He healed every disease known to man. He cast out demons. And He said you and I have the same power to do those things! Incredible!

But wait! Jesus wasn't finished. That was only half the verse. Don't be one of these people who takes Scripture out of context—read the whole verse! Read the verses around the verse. Learn the history. Know the context. Get the full story!

So here's the full story, the whole verse, as recorded in John's Gospel: "Very truly I tell you, whoever believes in me will do the works I have been doing, and they will do *even greater things* than these, because I am going to the Father" (John 14:12 NIV, emphasis added).

Jesus said that we who believe in Him will do the same powerful works that He has done. But not only that—we will do *even greater things*. Greater things! What could possibly be greater than turning water into wine and sack lunches into buffets, healing the sick and demon-possessed, calming storms and seeing people for who they really are?

So Jesus answered and said to them, "Have faith in God. For assuredly, I say to you, whoever says to this mountain, 'Be removed and be cast into the sea,' and does not doubt in his heart, but believes that those things he says will be done, he will have whatever he says. Therefore I say to you, whatever things you ask when you pray, believe that you receive them, and you will have them (Mark 11:22–24).

Jesus withered a fig tree, but He never cast a mountain into the sea. You could do that. You could do that if you believed you could. In fact, Jesus says you can do *anything* if you have faith and don't doubt.

There was a little congregation in the Great Smoky Mountains that built a new meeting house. Shortly before their dedication ceremony, the zoning committee said they couldn't open until they built a bigger parking lot. But they had built on every available inch of land. The only way they could enlarge the parking lot was to move the mountain. The pastor gathered those who had "mountain-moving faith" for a prayer meeting. The next morning a man from the next county over showed up and said he was looking for some fill dirt for a project they were building. Would the church be willing to let them cut into the mountain and take some dirt away? The construction crew took just enough for the church to enlarge their parking lot and open their doors on schedule.

Nothing could be clearer: faith moves mountains! And the supernatural power of God is available to every person who believes.

PRAYER

God, I believe in miracles. I have mountain-moving faith. No matter what troubles come my way, I come to you, in faith, believing that You have already planned my way of escape. To God be the glory! In Jesus' name; Amen!

THE HIGH PRIEST OF OUR CONFESSION

89

Therefore, brothers and sisters, holy partners in a heavenly calling, consider that Jesus, the apostle and high priest of our confession, was faithful to the one who appointed him, just as Moses also "was faithful in all God's house." Yet Jesus is worthy of more glory than Moses, just as the builder of a house has more honor than the house itself.

HEBREWS 3:1–3 NRSV

What is a proclamation in the Bible? The words to *proclaim* come from the Latin word meaning "to shout forth." When you hear someone say, "Hear ye! Hear ye!" that is a proclamation. A proclamation is a bold declaration, a clear statement of importance, a public announcement.

In the New Testament, there is a related word to proclaim, and that is *confess*. Confession is to "say the same as." So, for us as Bible believers, our confession of faith means that we say the words with our mouth that God has already said in His Word, which releases a supernatural force that can defeat anything in our life physically or spiritually.

An anointed proclamation is God's atomic bomb in the mouth of every believer. Your faith confession makes every demon in hell tremble. Your proclamation makes barriers to blessing fall like the walls of Jericho. Your confession of the Word conquers sickness and disease. Your confession and proclamation of the Word, in faith believing, will break every financial barrier and bring financial blessing that will take you from the pit to the palace. It's a Word from God that breaks a yoke. It's the Word that brings victory in our supernatural warfare. Your proclamation releases the authority of the living God into your situation, your battle, your crisis, your marriage, your business, and your health. It's the Word that brings complete victory. Without complete victory there is no victory. You cannot "kind of" win. You either do or you don't!

Proclamation and confession are critical

weapons in spiritual warfare. We are not in a fight just for the exercise. We're in the fight to win it! When you're in a spiritual combat, find a Bible verse that heaven gives you. Believe it, receive it, and make it your confession of faith—proclaim it!

According to Hebrews 3:1, Jesus is the High Priest of our confession. That means that Jesus releases His authority on what has been said when it lines up with the Word of God. So, whenever we confess what the Bible says, in faith believing that we have Jesus as our High Priest in heaven, the blessing comes to that confession. Jesus, your High Priest, gives your confession authority in heaven. And all heaven's power instantly attacks your problem, which is crushed by the power of the living God!

PRAYER

Jesus, High Priest of my confession, I make this proclamation, in faith believing: You are my light and salvation; whom shall I fear? You are the strength of my life; who have I to be afraid? I will not fear for Thou art with me. I will fight the good fight. I will finish the race. This is my good confession. In Jesus' name; Amen.

SECOND CHANCES

90

> "Come now,
> therefore, and
> I will send you
> to Pharaoh
> that you may
> bring My people,
> the children of
> Israel, out
> of Egypt."
>
> EXODUS 3:10

Moses was born shortly after Pharaoh placed a curse on the Israelites, condemning all newborn male children to death: "Every son who is born you shall cast into the river, and every daughter you shall save alive'" (Exodus 1:22). But Moses's mother was able to hide him for three months, before placing him in a basket and sending him down river with a hope and a prayer. Pharaoh's daughter discovered the little Hebrew baby, and named him Moses, saying, "I drew him out of the water" (Exodus 2:10).

Meanwhile, Pharaoh had enslaved the Hebrew people to work for him. One day, after Moses had grown, he saw an Egyptian beating one of the Hebrew workers. Thinking no one was watching, Moses killed the Egyptian and buried him in the sand. The next day, while trying to settle a dispute between two Hebrew men, it came out that someone had seen him kill the Egyptian. When Pharaoh found out, he tried to kill Moses, but Moses ran away, finding a home in the land of Midian.

But God wasn't done with Moses. God had a plan for him—a plan to use Moses to deliver the children of Israel out of Egypt and lead them into the Promised Land. But Moses would have to go back to face Pharaoh in order to fulfill his destiny. Get this: Moses was 80 years old when God called him back to Egypt, the place of his failure.

God has been talking to some of you about returning to the place where you failed, the place where you gave up on your dream. Maybe it was last year, or ten years ago, or 80. Maybe you were in high school, with a dream for your future that got derailed by a pregnancy. Maybe you were fresh out of college and faced rejection after rejection in the job market. Maybe you only wanted to be married, but that ended in divorce. Maybe as a young adult you heard God calling you into ministry or the mission field or to adopt, but you didn't heed His voice. Hear this: failure is not fatal. If it were, I would have been dead a long time ago. So, if you feel like you've been knocked down, run over, chewed up, spit out, and your life is meaningless, get up! God is calling you, just like He called to Moses. Victory is yours through Christ the Lord. Don't let your second chance pass you by!

PRAYER

God, I know that in You, failure is not fatal or final! Yes, there is a place in my past where I failed, there is a dream I gave up on, but You have redeemed my failures and restored my dreams. You have given me hope and a second chance.
I am getting up.
I am pressing in.
Victory is mine in Christ Jesus!
Amen.

THE ROD OF GOD

91

Then Moses took his wife and his sons and set them on a donkey, and he returned to the land of Egypt. And Moses took the rod of God in his hand.

EXODUS 4:20

Moses was 80 years old, a stutterer, a murderer, broken, and insecure beyond belief. But the Bible says in Psalm 51:17, "My sacrifice, O God, is a broken spirit; a broken and contrite heart you, God, will not despise" (NIV). God does not despise brokenness; God uses broken things!

God came to Moses in the burning bush and told him that He was going to use him to bring the Israelites out of Egypt and into the Promised Land. Moses was afraid that the people wouldn't listen to him,

> *So the Lord said to him, "What is that in your hand?" He said, "A rod." And He said, "Cast it on the ground." So he cast it on the ground, and it became a serpent; and Moses fled from it. Then the LORD said to Moses, "Reach out your hand and take it by the tail" (and he reached out his hand and caught it, and it became a rod in his hand), "that they may believe that the LORD God of their fathers, the God of Abraham, the God of Isaac, and the God of Jacob, has appeared to you"* (Exodus 4:2–5).

What Moses had in his hand was just an ordinary stick, but there was potential in that ordinary stick that Moses had never imagined. God can use anything that will surrender itself to His service. Don't ever consider yourself useless in the Kingdom of God. A man who stuttered and carried a crooked stick led two-million people out of Pharaoh's bondage and established the nation of Israel. Just imagine what God could do through you!

If you analyze Moses's ministry, every time supernatural power was needed, God's divine authority was released through that rod. When Moses arrived in Pharaoh's court, he cast down the rod and it became a snake again. Jannes and Jambres, two warlocks, threw down their staffs and they became snakes also. Two snakes against one. But Moses's snake ate the other two snakes. At the Red Sea, when Pharaoh's chariots were thundering across the desert in hot pursuit, when the waters of the Red Sea needed to be divided, Moses lifted that rod, put it in the water and the waters split, allowing them to walk across on dry land. When the Egyptian army pursued the Jewish people, Moses held up that rod again, and the water swallowed the Egyptians up. When the children of Israel needed water, Moses struck a rock with that staff, and the rock produced enough water for millions of people and their livestock. Every time Moses held that staff, supernatural things happened. The only thing that Moses needed for 40 years of miracle ministry was one shepherd's rod.

You have the rod of God. It is the Word of God, the Bible. It is the only instrument you need to defeat the powers and principalities of darkness. It is supernatural. It contains unlimited power. It is alive. It is anointed. It is sharper than any two-edged sword. And the words within it are spoken under the supernatural anointing of the Holy Spirit.

PRAYER

Father, thank You that You have given me a rod, Your Word. It is alive and active, sharper than a two-edged sword. With Your Word at my disposal, I have unlimited power through the supernatural anointing of the Holy Spirit! In Jesus' name; Amen!

THE MIRACLE IN YOUR MOUTH

92

If you abide in Me, and My words abide in you, you will ask what you desire, and it shall be done for you.

JOHN 15:7

What abides in you? God's Word. And His Word is like a miracle in your mouth. On the morning of creation, God's anointed Word was released, and the universe was spoken into existence. Yet the greatest demonstration of God's spoken Word is still to come, in the battle of Armageddon:

> *Now I saw heaven opened, and behold, a white horse. And He who sat on him was called Faithful and True, and in righteousness He judges and makes war. His eyes were like a flame of fire, and on His head were many crowns. He had a name written that no one knew except Himself. He was clothed with a robe dipped in blood, and His name is called **The Word of God**. And the armies in heaven, clothed in fine linen, white and clean, followed Him on white horses. Now **out of His mouth goes a sharp sword**, that with it He should strike the nations. And He Himself will rule them with a rod of iron. He Himself treads the winepress of the fierceness and wrath of Almighty God. And He has on His robe and on His thigh a name written: KING OF KINGS AND LORD OF LORDS (Revelation 19:11–16, emphasis added).*

An invasion is coming from heaven and His name is Jesus. The two-edged sword—the spoken Word of God—will smite the nations. Why? Because the nations were created by the spoken Word of God. Psalm 149 says, "Let the high praises of God be in their mouth" (v. 6). The miracle is in your mouth! And it will bring life and healing to those who speak it.

> My son, give attention to my words; incline your ear to my sayings. Do not let them depart from your eyes; keep them in the midst of your heart; for they are life to those who find them, and health to all their flesh (Proverbs 4:20–22).

> Then they cried out to the LORD in their trouble, and He saved them out of their distresses. He sent His word and healed them, and delivered them from their destructions (Psalm 107:19–20).

> Pleasant words are like a honeycomb, sweetness to the soul and health to the bones (Proverbs 16:24).

Pleasant speaking brings health to your bones. That's not a metaphor, that's a fact! Information without application produces frustration. Until you light the fuse on the stick of dynamite, all you have is a lifeless package. The same is true for the Word of God. You can read it, you can store it up in your heart, you can bind it to your wrists and write it on your forehead; but until you boldly proclaim it, you won't see its fruit. There is a miracle in your mouth—confess it out loud!

PRAYER

Father God, You have set before me life and death. I choose life. You have set before me blessing and cursing. I choose blessing. I will not fear, for You are with me. Your Word is my strength, my fortress, my high tower. My body is the temple of the Holy Spirit. I praise You and give You thanks. I will declare Your greatness and bless Your name forever. In Jesus' name; Amen.

MIRACLE-WORKING POWER

93

*And as you
go, preach,
saying, "The
kingdom of
heaven is at
hand." Heal
the sick, cleanse
the lepers, raise
the dead, cast
out demons.
Freely you have
received,
freely give.*

MATTHEW 10:7–8

Look at the healing miracles of Jesus. He healed
the lame. He healed the deaf. He healed the blind.
On one occasion, He healed with one touch. On
another, He touched twice. On a third occasion,
He mixed spit with mud in His hand and put it
in the eyes of a blind man. He healed the paralytic who had a seizure disorder. He healed blood
disease. He healed leprosy. That means He can
heal AIDS, cancer, anything that ails you. Medical
science may not have caught up yet, there may be
no "cure" for what you have, but I assure you of
this: there is no disease that is greater than God's
healing power! The nail-pierced hand of Jesus
Christ, the Great Physician, can heal your body!

*The blind see and the lame walk; the lepers
are cleansed and the deaf hear; the dead
are raised up and the poor have the gospel
preached to them* (Matthew 11:5).

Jesus healed from a distance. He healed the
centurion's servant and the Roman official's son,
both were a long way off from the servant and the
son, and at the same hour that these men came
to Jesus in prayer. Jesus healed one-on-one. He
healed in mass. He healed every day of the week.

*And behold, there was a man who had a
withered hand. And they asked Him, saying,
"Is it lawful to heal on the Sabbath?"—that
they might accuse Him. Then He said to
them, "What man is there among you who
has one sheep, and if it falls into a pit on the
Sabbath, will not lay hold of it and lift it out?
Of how much more value then is a man than
a sheep? Therefore it is lawful to do good*

on the Sabbath." Then He said to the man, "Stretch out your hand." And he stretched it out, and it was restored as whole as the other (Matthew 12:10–13).

Jesus not only healed, but He transferred His healing power to His disciples: "And when He had called His twelve disciples to Him, He gave them power over unclean spirits, to cast them out, and to heal all kinds of sickness and all kinds of disease" (Matthew 10:1). So much healing power did the disciples have, that people were healed just by touching their shadows.

And through the hands of the apostles many signs and wonders were done among the people. And they were all with one accord in Solomon's Porch. Yet none of the rest dared join them, but the people esteemed them highly. And believers were increasingly added to the Lord, multitudes of both men and women, so that they brought the sick out into the streets and laid them on beds and couches, that at least the shadow of Peter passing by might fall on some of them. Also a multitude gathered from the surrounding cities to Jerusalem, bringing sick people and those who were tormented by unclean spirits, and they were all healed (Acts 5:12–16).

"… and they were ALL healed!" That, my friend, is miracle-working power!

PRAYER

God, I believe in miracles. I believe in Your supernatural power that is at work in the world. I believe in Your ministry of healing. I believe that You have the power to change my life with a touch, a word, a look, a shadow. I receive that healing, in Jesus' name! Amen.

A REAL MIRACLE

94

Because you have made the LORD, who is my refuge, even the Most High, your dwelling place, no evil shall befall you, nor shall any plague come near your dwelling; for He shall give His angels charge over you, to keep you in all your ways. In their hands they shall bear you up, lest you dash your foot against a stone.

PSALM 91:9–12

In December 1971, a demonized man walked into my church with a gun in his hand. He stopped just ten feet in front of where I was standing, leading our Wednesday night Bible study. He stood right there and said, "I've come to kill you in front of your congregation to prove that Satan has more power than Jesus Christ."

In God's strength and power, I said, "The Bible declares that no weapon forged against me shall prosper."

He said, "I have a gun."

I said, "I have the Word of God."

He proceeded to tell me he was going to kill me on the count of three. One ... Two ... Bang! He lied. He never made it to three. He started shooting when he got to the count of two. He emptied the gun of its bullets from ten feet away, and he missed me with every shot.

Psalm 91:11 says, "For He shall give His angels charge over you, to keep you in all your ways." The angels of God that protect the righteous were deflecting those shots. There's no other explanation. It was an absolute miracle from God!

It is important to note that God brings miracles and He will send His angels to protect you, but He doesn't want to be tested. I didn't seek out a gunfight to prove that God could save me. I didn't ask the man to shoot me to prove that God would be my shield and buckler. God will show up, but He does not want to be provoked.

Remember the scene when Jesus is being tempted by Satan in the desert. Satan knew that Jesus hadn't had anything to eat or drink, so his first temptation was to Jesus' carnal nature. To which Jesus replied: "Man shall not live by bread alone" (Matthew 4:4). For his second temptation, Satan tried a little harder:

> Then the devil took Him up into the holy city, set Him on the pinnacle of the temple, and said to Him, "If You are the Son of God, throw Yourself down. For it is written: 'He shall give His angels charge over you,' and, 'In their hands they shall bear you up, lest you dash your foot against a stone.'" Jesus said to him, "It is written again, 'You shall not tempt the LORD your God.'" (Matthew 4:5–7).

Satan knows the Scriptures. He knows the psalm that says God will send His angels to watch over you, and he will use it to try to tempt us to test that power. But Jesus knows the Scriptures, too. And He knows that God is not to be tempted.

PRAYER

God, I am growing in my faith so that I don't have to see it to believe it. Your miracles are at work all around me. Your hand of protection is there at a moment's notice. You are my shield and buckler; I will not be afraid. In Jesus' name; Amen.

GOD'S MEDICARE PROGRAM

95

*Bless the LORD,
O my soul;
and all that is
within me, bless
His holy name!
Bless the Lord,
O my soul, and
forget not all
His benefits:
who forgives all
your iniquities,
who heals all
your diseases,
who redeems
your life from
destruction, who
crowns you with
lovingkindness
and tender
mercies, who
satisfies your
mouth with good
things, so that
your youth is
renewed like the
eagle's.*

PSALM 103:1–5

David writes in Psalm 103 about God's benefits. What are His benefits? The first on David's list is: "who forgives all of your iniquities" (v. 3). What is an iniquity? An iniquity is a sin that you know is a sin, but you do it anyway. (Ouch!) Verse three continues with, "who heals all your diseases." Notice the connection that is made between the spiritual and the physical. Man has a twofold nature. He is both physical and spiritual. And both natures are equally addressed in this Scripture. Your physical body is exposed to disease, and your soul is corrupted by sin. The plan of redemption makes it possible for your sins to be forgiven and your body to be healed.

Notice in verse three that God forgives ALL your iniquities and heals ALL your diseases. David didn't say "some," he said "all." I think people get the idea that it's easy for God to heal a head cold, but they think He can't touch cancer. Let me tell you: cancer is not a challenge for God. When you have the faith for it, you can move mountains. "And whatever you ask in My name, that I will do, that the Father may be glorified in the Son" (John 14:13). God is just waiting for you to uncross your fingers and start believing!

The first promise of healing to the Jewish people leaving Egypt is made in Exodus 15:26, "I will put none of the diseases on you which I have brought on the Egyptians. For I am the LORD who heals you." Just how successful was God's Medicare program for the children of Israel? David answered in Psalm 105:37, "... there was none feeble among His tribes." Two million people lived for 40 years without a head cold, because God gave them perfect health!

Do you need a miracle? When you want what you've never had, you've got to do what you've never done. Have faith in God—not just faith that God exists or that the Bible is true, but faith that the things God did in the Bible, He will do for you, and do it now. That's faith!

PRAYER

Lord, I have a miracle mentality. I expect You to do miracles in my life and thank You for them. I receive Your supernatural healing in my body through good physical health. I receive Your supernatural healing in my spirit through the forgiveness of my sins and iniquities. I believe that New Testament, powerful, life-changing, healing faith has never been withdrawn and neither has Your miracle-working power! In Jesus' name; Amen.

THE SUBSTITUTE

96

*Then Aaron
shall cast lots
for the two
goats: one lot
for the LORD
and the other
lot for the
scapegoat.*

LEVITICUS 16:8

In ancient Israel, at the time of national repentance, the priest would kill one goat, dip his fingers in the blood and smear it on the head of the second goat. The second goat was the "scapegoat"—the substitute for the people's sins. The scapegoat carried all the sins and sicknesses of Israel, and they cast that goat right off a cliff. Then, for good measure, they threw a rock on top of the scapegoat to guarantee it was dead. When the goat was "officially" dead, the sins of Israel had been completely forgiven for that year.

An unforgettable story in Scripture is that of Abraham and his son, Isaac. Isaac was born to Abraham when Abraham was 100 years old. Who knows what it's like to wait that long for your prayers to be answered? Anyone? Because Abraham had waited so long, God thought it wise to test him, to make sure he hadn't begun to worship the answer to his prayers over the One who had brought the answer. So, God told Abraham to take his beloved son to the land of Moriah and offer him there as a sacrifice. Along the way,

> *Isaac spoke to Abraham his father and said, "My father!" And he said, "Here I am, my son." Then he said, "Look, the fire and the wood, but where is the lamb for a burnt offering?" And Abraham said, "My son, God will provide for Himself the lamb for a burnt offering." So the two of them went together* (Genesis 22:7–8).

"... God will provide for Himself the lamb." Abraham believed those words in his heart of hearts and they came true. With Isaac bound to the altar and the knife above his head, God called to Abraham and said, "Wait! You passed the test! I know you fear Me, so look over there and you will see a ram in the thicket—a substitute for your son."

> ... So Abraham went and took the ram, and offered it up for a burnt offering instead of his son. And Abraham called the name of the place, The-LORD-Will-Provide; as it is said to this day, "In the Mount of the LORD it shall be provided" (Genesis 22:13–14).

It is an unforgettable story, but it is not the greatest story of substitution ever told. Isaiah 53:4 says: "Surely He has borne our griefs and carried our sorrows; yet we esteemed Him stricken, smitten by God, and afflicted." Look at the two words, "borne" and "carried." They denote more than sympathy. They represent actual substitution. They represent the absolute removal of the thing talked about. When Jesus, on the Cross, cried, "It is finished," He carried our sins away; He carried our sicknesses away; He carried our heartache away. He is our burden bearer. He is our scapegoat at Calvary.

PRAYER

Father, thank You, that because of Your Son, death has no power over me, sickness has no power over me. Jesus, at the Cross of Calvary, carried it all away for me. He has borne it and He has delivered me once and for all time! In Jesus' name; Amen.

THE GOD WHO HEALED YESTERDAY IS STILL HEALING TODAY

97

"And these signs will follow those who believe: In My name they will cast out demons; they will speak with new tongues; they will take up serpents; and if they drink anything deadly, it will by no means hurt them; they will lay hands on the sick, and they will recover."

MARK 16:17–18

In Mark 16, Jesus gives the "Great Commission" to the 11 remaining disciples: "Go into all the world and preach the gospel to every creature" (v. 15). But He isn't done talking. He tells the 11 the "signs" to look for, to know who has responded to the Gospel and become a believer, and who hasn't:

> *He who believes and is baptized will be saved; but he who does not believe will be condemned. And these signs will follow those who believe: In My name they will cast out demons; they will speak with new tongues; they will take up serpents; and if they drink anything deadly, it will by no means hurt them; they will lay hands on the sick, and they will recover"* (vv. 16–18).

These "signs" aren't limited to Jesus. They aren't even limited to the disciples. They are the signs of ALL believers—casting out demons, speaking in tongues, taking up serpents, laying hands on the sick. The point is, miracles did not end with the disciples! It is still God's will for us to lay hands on the sick and for them to recover.

> *Is anyone among you sick? Let him call for the elders of the church, and let them pray over him, anointing him with oil in the name of the Lord. And the prayer of faith will save the sick, and the Lord will raise him up. And if he has committed sins, he will be forgiven* (James 5:14–15).

Notice to whom this power is given. It is

not given to Peter, James, and John, but to the elders of the church. Every church that existed had elders, as most churches in America have elders. And one of the responsibilities of an elder is to have enough of God in them that they can anoint with oil; "the prayer of faith shall save the sick, and the Lord shall raise him [them] up!"

Hebrews 13:8 says, "Jesus Christ is the same yesterday, today, and forever." This is an echo of the voice of Jesus that said, "Lo, I am with you always, even to the end of the age" (Matthew 28:20). His presence has never been withdrawn from us. His love has never been withdrawn from us. His grace has never been withdrawn from us. His power to heal, save, deliver, and set captives free has never diminished. He is the same yesterday, today, and forever. Therefore, the God who healed yesterday is still healing today and will be until the millennial Kingdom!

PRAYER

Thank You, Father, that the same power that raised Christ from the dead gives life to my mortal body through Your Spirit, who dwells in me. My soul prospers and I am in good health thanks to Your Spirit at work within me! In Jesus' name; Amen.

EIGHT STEPS TO RECEIVING YOUR MIRACLE

98

"But you shall receive power when the Holy Spirit has come upon you; and you shall be witnesses to Me in Jerusalem, and in all Judea and Samaria, and to the end of the earth."

ACTS 1:8

There is no "quick fix" that will take you up out of your storm; but I do believe that if you follow these eight steps you will be headed in the right direction:

1. The confession of sin. Psalm 66:18 says, "If I had not confessed the sin in my heart, the Lord would not have listened" (NLT). When you confess your sins, God's ears are opened.

2. Recognize it is God's will to heal you. "Beloved, I pray that you may prosper in all things and be in health, just as your soul prospers" (3 John 1:2). God's desire is that you be healthy and whole!

3. Expect a miracle. Remember, faith is not believing that God *can*, faith is believing that God *will*.

4. Activate God's healing power by the Word of God. Proverbs 3 encourages you to keep God's commands, to bind them around your neck, and write them on the tablet of your heart, for "it shall be health to thy navel, and marrow to thy bones" (v. 8, KJV). A baby's source of life is in the navel. The marrow of your bones is where blood cells are created, which carry oxygen to your body and help fight and prevent disease. So, Proverbs is saying that the Word of God is the Source of Life. When you need health and healing, read Proverbs 3, because it will restore and refresh you!

5. Accept that your healing was paid for at the Cross: "... by his wounds we are healed" (Isaiah 53:5, NIV). Don't crawl down the

aisle of a cathedral and kiss the toe of Saint Peter trying to get healed. It's a waste of time. Healing is already yours!

6. Act upon your faith. To Moses, God said, cast down your rod. To Elijah, pour 12 barrels of water on the sacrifice at Mount Carmel. To the man with the withered hand, Jesus said to "stretch out your hand" (Matthew 12:13). To the man lying by the pool, Jesus said, "Rise, take up your bed and walk" (John 5:8). God wants to see your faith in action. Put your faith to work (see James 2:26)!

7. Denounce the kingdom of darkness. Jesus did not interview demons, He cast them out (see Matthew 8:16). If you're trying to have a conversation with the devil, stop it! If you really have God in you, demons will fear you and flee from you.

8. Recognize that healing comes on the wings of the Holy Spirit (see Romans 8:11). God, the Father, wills it. Jesus, the Son, paid for it at the Cross, and the Holy Spirit brings it. The Holy Spirit is crucial to the healing process. If you're rejecting the Holy Spirit, you're short-stopping God's ability to work miracles in your life. In an atmosphere of praise and worship, the Holy Spirit comes down and people are healed without anyone touching them. God's power moves like an ocean wave. It is supernatural and it is powerful.

PRAYER

Heavenly Father, today I need a miracle. I need for the impossible to become possible. Now Heavenly Father, in the presence of the Holy Spirit, I receive your miracle-working power. It's mine. Through the power of Your Word, through the death of Jesus, and in faith, I receive it now. In Jesus' name; Amen.

THE ERA OF MIRACLES IS NOT OVER

99

So Jesus answered and said to them, "Assuredly, I say to you, if you have faith and do not doubt, you will not only do what was done to the fig tree, but also if you say to this mountain, 'Be removed and be cast into the sea,' it will be done. And whatever things you ask in prayer, believing, you will receive."

MATTHEW 21:21–22

Do you know how to receive a miracle? Do you know how to recognize a miracle? Do you reject the reality of miracles? A man once came to me and said, "I don't believe in miracles." I said, "Sooner or later you're going to need one. When that time comes, then you'll believe!"

The era of miracles is not over. Hebrews 13:8 says that "Jesus Christ is the same yesterday, today, and forever." What He did by the shores of the Sea of Galilee, He can do in your cities, towns, homes, schools, and offices today. Our Father, who art in heaven, is still *Jehovah Rophe*, the Lord Who heals all disease. His Son, Jesus Christ, is still the Great Physician. He is the Balm of Gilead. He is the conqueror of death, hell, and the grave. He calls the stars by name. He has numbered the hairs on your head. He has not forgotten you. He knows where you are. He knows how you are. He knows what you need. Ask, believe, and you shall receive.

In Matthew 9, Jesus heals two blind men with these words: "Do you believe that I am able to do this? ... According to your faith let it be to you" (vv. 28–29). He has the same words for you today. Do you believe that He is able to heal you, your relationships, emotions, bank account, and broken heart? "According to your faith" you will be healed! But by your lack of faith you will remain in captivity. Matthew 21:22 says, "If you believe, you will receive whatever you ask for in prayer" (NIV). You must believe it to receive it!

Do you know the God of miracles? Do you know His miracle-working power? Do you know that He is the same yesterday, today, and forever?

For those of you who need healing, whether it be in your heart, soul, mind, or your body, I pray: Be healed in your emotions. Be healed in your memories. Be healed in your physical body. Be healed in your marriage. Be healed in your finances. Be healed from your broken heart. Be healed from your addiction. Be healed from your inferiority complex. Be healed from your lack of confidence. Rejoice and be exceedingly glad. You are a child of the King, so live like it! Talk like it! Act like it! You are free, in Jesus' name, if you just believe!

PRAYER

Lord, You are the same yesterday, today, and forever. You are the Balm of Gilead. You answer prayers. You set captives free. You are my Redeemer, my Savior, my Friend. You are everything I need. I am a child of the King! In Jesus' name; Amen.

CONCLUSION: YOU ARE MORE THAN A CONQUEROR

100

Yet in all these things we are more than conquerors through Him who loved us.

ROMANS 8:37

Welcome to day 100! Congratulations! You made it!

Over the past 100 days you have faced fears, failures, sin, sickness, and disease. You have looked rejection and resentment right in the face. You have conquered insecurities. And you have triumphed over trials with the joy of the Lord, the peace that passes understanding, by rejoicing in all things (again I say, rejoice!), and releasing the miracle that is in your mouth.

You have come to see that you can be blessed by tribulation and laugh the devil right off the pedestal he put himself on! You have seen how God shows His strength through Creation and nature; He is your strength in weakness and a shelter in your storm. He has been the Healer to your sickness, the Deliverer to your oppression, the Friend when you were lonely, the Provider of your every need. He has given you reason to dream again. You have learned the power of His Word in your mouth. You now know without a doubt that you have no reason to fear, because He is with you, His rod and His staff comfort you. Even when it feels like no one else understands, you have a High Priest who understands your suffering and who appeals to heaven on your behalf. And nothing—I repeat NOTHING!—can separate you from the love that is in Christ Jesus our Lord.

Today, we celebrate His goodness and His mercy. We celebrate our redemption. We celebrate our healing. We celebrate that we are kings and queens unto God, that we are ambassadors of Christ; the royal blood of heaven is flowing in our veins. Because of Jesus Christ, all of this is possible and nothing is impossible. Everything that we ask in His name is ours. When we knock, He answers. When we cry out, He hears and responds. When we cast our cares on Him, He carries them. When we confess and forsake our sins, He removes them as far as the east is from the west, never to be remembered any more.

Storms will come. He assures us of this. But when they do, you will be ready. And this time you won't just barely make it through. You won't be sinking in the storm while Jesus is asleep in the boat. You will be resting sweetly beside Him with a smile on your face because you are MORE than a conqueror in Christ Jesus. You are STORM PROOF.

PRAYER

Father, thank You that You have made me storm proof! In Jesus' name; Amen.

PASTOR JOHN HAGEE

Pastor John C. Hagee is the founder and Senior Pastor of Cornerstone Church in San Antonio, Texas, a non-denominational evangelical church with more than 22,000 active members. Pastor Hagee has served the Lord in the gospel ministry for over 60 years.

Pastor Hagee received a Bachelor of Science degree from Southwestern Assemblies of God University in Waxahachie, Texas and a second Bachelor of Science degree from Trinity University in San Antonio, Texas. He earned his Master's Degree in Educational Administration from the University of North Texas in Denton, Texas.

He has received Honorary Doctorates from Oral Roberts University, Canada Christian College, and Netanya Academic College of Israel.

Pastor Hagee is the author of 40 major books, seven of which were on *The New York Times* Best Seller's List.

He is the founder of *Hagee Ministries*, which telecasts his teachings throughout America and the nations of the world. Over the years, *Hagee Ministries* has given more than $100 million toward humanitarian causes in Israel.

Pastor Hagee is the founder of Cornerstone Christian Schools that just completed a $100 million dollar campus which holds 2,400 students and is committed to the Bible-based education of the future generation.

He is the founder of the *Sanctuary of Hope*, a multi-million dollar facility that gives young, pregnant mothers a home to live in and raise their children rather than aborting them. This home gives the opportunity of life to children that would have otherwise been killed in abortion clinics.

Pastor Hagee is the founder and National Chairman of *Christians United For Israel* (CUFI), a grass-roots organization which has grown to become the largest Christian pro-Israel group in the

United States with over 7 million members that speak as one voice on behalf of Israel.

John Hagee was recognized by the state of Israel on its 70th Anniversary as one of the 70 greatest contributors to Israel since statehood. He was also invited by U.S. Ambassador David Friedman to give the benediction at the opening of the U.S. Embassy in Jerusalem.

Pastor Hagee and his wife Diana are blessed with five children and thirteen grandchildren.